Benjamin Dawson

Free Thoughts on the Subject of a Farther Reformation

of the Church of England

Benjamin Dawson

Free Thoughts on the Subject of a Farther Reformation
of the Church of England

ISBN/EAN: 9783337002725

Printed in Europe, USA, Canada, Australia, Japan

Cover: Foto ©Lupo / pixelio.de

More available books at **www.hansebooks.com**

FREE THOUGHTS

ON THE SUBJECT OF

A FARTHER REFORMATION

OF THE

CHURCH of ENGLAND;

FREE THOUGHTS

ON THE SUBJECT OF

A FARTHER REFORMATION

OF THE

CHURCH of ENGLAND;

In SIX NUMBERS:

TO WHICH ARE ADDED,

The REMARKS of the EDITOR.

By the AUTHOR of
A short and safe EXPEDIENT for terminating the present Debates about SUBSCRIPTION.

Published by BENJAMIN DAWSON, L.L.D.
Rector of Burgh, in Suffolk.

LONDON:
Printed for J. WILKIE, Nº 71, St. Paul's-church-yard.

M.DCC.LXXI. 7

PREFACE.

IF an apology for the appearance of the following sheets should seem on any account requisite, it can only be, that the subject of them has already been sufficiently discussed. Some may think it has been persued to an unnecessary, as well as wearisome length. Certain it is, the case of subscription to human articles of religious faith and doctrine, had received from the author of the Confessional *so ample and satisfactory an examination, that the controversy occasioned by that signal performance, has served rather to try, and, in the issue, to confirm the validity of the learned writer's arguments, than to throw any additional light upon the subject. This, however, doth not supersede either the propriety or the utility of a farther communication of the sentiments of learned and liberal-minded men, as occasion may offer.*

The end of the controversy, it should be remembered, is the improvement of our ecclesiastical establishment, more particularly in the removal of those restraints upon religious freedom, which were unhappily admitted into it at the first, and are suffered to continue in it, though evidently to its discredit and disadvantage, if not immediate danger. Towards this desirable end much new information on the head of subscription, can neither

A

be

be neceſſary, nor is now to be expected; yet
pertinent remarks from ſome, free and ſpi-
rited, but decent and reſpectful remonſtrances
from others, and the endeavours of all the
friends of religious truth and freedom to excite
attention to the original principles of proteſ-
tantiſm, may contribute much, and are become
more ſeaſonable and needful than ever. A man-
ly avowal itſelf of our attachment to the cauſe
of reformation, may have conſiderable influence:
And I know not but that ſteadily to countenance
it only in this way, on every fair occaſion, in
the face of a moſt unreaſonable and perverſe
oppoſition, may be more conducive to its ſucceſs,
than the brighteſt diſplay of mere literary abilities in its favour, or even the cleareſt deciſion
in the way of debate.

It is not ſo much to convince our adverſaries
(they appear not to have wanted conviction)
as to prevent their ſophiſtry from taking effect
upon the minds of others better affected to reformation, that we have undertaken to con-
fute them: And therefore, we are unwilling to
ſtop ſhort at this point, honourable as it is to
have gained it. The trueſt glory remains ſtill
to be merited (reaped it cannot be here) by
uniformly perſiſting through life in the ſup-
port, and contributing, to the utmoſt of our
abilities, and in the free uſe of all lawful,
honeſt, and Chriſtian means, towards the ſucceſs of the cauſe we have engaged in.

How

PREFACE.

How far the Work now submitted to the inspection of the Public is calculated to answer the Editor's intention in its appearance, signified by the foregoing considerations, must be left to the judgement of the same Public. With that intention there will be no doubt of its having been penned. Every page manifests the earnest desire of the Writer to serve the interests of religious truth, and, in subservience to that noblest end, his zeal in behalf of farther reformation in the church. The plain, easy, unaffected manner, in which he delivers his own, and introduces the opinions and observations of others, is almost peculiar to himself, and well worthy of imitation. His uncommon candour in interpreting the obnoxious passages which occur in the writings of those he animadverts upon, cannot escape the notice of his readers, nor fail to meet with general esteem and approbation. This amiable quality in our Author has been remarked on a former occasion *. I am almost tempted — yet not of an uncandid spirit, I trust — to add, that he possesses it, if it were possible, in the extreme. It cannot altoge-

---

* See the Preface to, A SHORT and SAFE EXPEDIENT for terminating the present debates about SUBSCRIPTIONS.

ther

PREFACE.

ther be approved, if it lead him to lofe an advantage to the caufe of truth, by forbearing fufficiently to expofe the fpirit and views of its opponents in certain inftances.

In laying this work before the Public, it might hardly be reckoned fair dealing to fupprefs the circumftance of its being a pofthumous one; and, on another hand, to declare it, is but to do juftice to the reputation of the deceafed, in whofe behalf the Editor puts in thereby a reafonable claim to fome indulgence and allowance for thofe defects, which his own Remarks may be thought but poorly to fupply. To add them, however, feemed not improper, as the Author had fignified his intention, not only of requefting me to undertake this publication for him, but alfo of fubmitting the manufcripts to my infpection, and for my free fentiments, previous to the final revifion of them for the Prefs.

BENJAMIN DAWSON.

Burgh, Auguft 20, 1771.

CON-

CONTENTS.

CONTENTS.

Advertisement.

The Reader is desired to take Notice, that the small Figures, ',',',' &c. refer to the *Editor's Remarks*, which begin at page 133.

ERRATA

E R R A T A.

Pag. 20. l. 24. for *of*, read *if*.
144. l. 28. for *in* anſwer, read *in an* ANSWER.

FREE THOUGHTS, &c.

N°. I.

Modern Church-Policy:

CONTAINING

Articles of opinion and subscription, formed upon the plan of the Alliance *between Church and State, and more particularly collected from the sermon of Dr.* Balguy *upon the subject.*

I. Scripture.

"THE bare words of *Scripture* will never enable us to resolve that variety of doubts and scruples (some of considerable importance) to which we shall find ourselves exposed, in relation

B   to

to church-authority *. Even the ableſt critics have waſted their time and pains in this unprofitable ſearch; where neither ſkill in languages, nor knowledge of antiquity, could contribute any thing to their ſucceſs.

" An accurate deſcription of men's rights and duties [in this inſtance] is not to be found in ſcripture. The knowledge of theſe is ſuppoſed, not taught by the ſacred writers. The bible was never intended for ſuch purpoſes.——The directions of the founders of our holy religion

---

* In other words, *church-authority* is totally of *political* inſtitution. Which is giving up the long conteſted point at once, and, in effect, the text into the bargain ¹.—Nor is this all: The partizans of *Rome* are not ſo much out in their reckoning, when they aſſert,

That the Scriptures are obſcure, and hard to be underſtood, even in things neceſſary. That it belongeth not to all the faithful to ſearch into the meaning of the Scripture. That you cannot know the ſenſe of the Scripture without the interpretation of the church. That the Scripture hath no authority but from the church. That the Scripture is not a ſufficient rule for faith without tradition. That if any one ſhall offer to prove his opinion by the Scriptures, he muſt be flatly told, that Scripture-arguments are of no avail in theological diſputes; which muſt reſt only on church-authority, and be decided by it. Finally, That the Scriptures are dead characters, a dead letter, an unſenſed letter, a ſhell without kernel, a delphic ſword, a leaden rule, a ſhoe fit for any foot, a noſe of wax, that may be moulded into any ſhape, and made a ſubject of debate and contention without end.

to

to us are, for the moſt part, very general. Even their example muſt be cau-
tiouſly urged, in different times, and under different circumſtances."

II. *Church* and *church-authority.*

" A church is a number of perſons agree-
ing to unite in public aſſemblies for the
performance of religious duties *, *viz.*
public inſtruction, and public worſhip.—
Conſidered as an inſtitution merely human
(in which light alone we now ſurvey it)
the divinity of its origin is a circumſtance
of no moment [1].—The firſt ſketch of church-
authority, is a power in the ſociety of ap-
pointing its miniſters. This implies an ex-
cluſion of others from the miniſterial office; which none can undertake without
ſuch appointment: and if any man ſhall
oppoſe the perſons who are appointed lawfully for this office, he renders himſelf in-
capable of continuing a member of this

---

* I have looked into a conſiderable number of our beſt
Engliſh divines, to ſee under what characters they deſcribe
the Chriſtian church in general, or (which muſt have the
ſame eſſentials) a Chriſtian church in particular, and do not
find any one of them all, from the reformation downward,
who deſcribes either church * in that vague and indiſcrimi-
nate manner, that this modern doctor does.

politi-

political fociety or church; and is therefore
liable to be excommunicated.—Yet ftill it
muft be obferved, that a church thus
framed, cannot fupport her power by *civil
fanctions*. She can only take away what
fhe herfelf has given."

III. *Minifters of religion.*

" EVERY form of religion requires attention and ftudy in thofe who are to teach
it *. Religion muft be made a profeffion, or
no man will be at leifure to learn and to
teach it; nor will he give his time in
teaching it to the public, unlefs excited by
public rewards '. Nor can any minifter of-
ficiating in a fociety, invefted with a power
to prefcribe the forms of its public offices,
depart in any refpect from the public inftitution, much lefs act in contradiction to
it, without ufurping a power not committed to him. If he does this, and much
more, if (without any pretence to infpiration) he lives in open war with the national church, of which he profeffes himfelf a minifter; he violates the truft repofed
in him; he acts contrary to the moft evident principles of juftice and honour, and
fo renders himfelf unfit to be trufted. The
confequence, deprivation from his office,
and

and from the rewards attending it; [and, in fome cafes, excommunication alfo *.]

' " THERE is no neceffity that the mini-fters of religion fhould be appointed by the people; and much expedience in a different method of appointment. To thofe who are authorized to govern the church, muft be committed the care of chufing *fit* perfons for difcharging the offices of religion †.

---

* See the canons, and cafes in the law-books.—But can it be affirmed upon the *principles of juftice and honour*, and with the leaft degree of common civility and candor, that any of our eftablifhed minifters in thefe days, launch out into any of thefe high crimes and mifdemeanours, for which they are to be fo feverely treated ? It may deferve notice, that among the hoftilities fuppofed to be raifed by clergymen againft the church, immoralities, the moft dangerous acts of *open war* againft it, are not mentioned. Happy for this church, if there be no delinqnents in *this* kind, who continue unmolefted to *take her wages !* Are not fuch as thefe, if any fuch there be, in *actual fervice againft her ?* And can there be any comparifon between the actual mifchief done by thefe to the church, and the fincere kindnefs and honour fo evidently intended to be done to her, by thofe who with all proper decency, humility and modefty, do only petition for a revifal of fuch particulars as manifeftly call for amendments in her ?—Thefe, it feems, are not to be *pitied*, when they cannot be *confuted*. To this clafs of men, the plea for *compaffion*, it feems, will not extend. *Serm.* p. 19, 20.

† But what if lay-patrons fhould prefent to them *unfit* perfons ? And fhould follow their ftroke with a *Qu. impedit ?*

B 3

IV.

IV. *Uniformity: Separation.*

" It is the bufinefs of perfons appointed
to govern the church *, to prefcribe the
rules and forms of public religion. It is
of the higheft importance to the interefts of
religion, that it fhould be confiftent and
uniform in its outward appearance.<. Without uniformity, public inftitutions can never obtain their full effect. The variety of
religious forms fhakes and fubverts the belief of all religion.

" Men fhould be careful not to break
the uniformity of public religion. Nothing
lefs than the moft effential interefts of religion and virtue will juftify a *feparation.*—
The people are not at liberty, while they
remain in fociety, to defert at pleafure their
lawful paftors, and flock in crowds to receive inftruction from thofe who have no
authority to give it. If they cannot lawfully
comply with the terms of communion, let
them make an open *feparation.* The community has no kind or degree of power
over thofe who care not to continue members of it; nor to caufe them to profefs

---

* See the next article.

them-

themfelves members of a church, which they confcientioufly difobey."

V. *Authority of the civil magiftrate in matters of religion.*

" IT greatly concerns the public peace and fafety, that all church-authority fhould be under the controul of the civil governor 7 : that religious affemblies, as well as others, fhould be fubject to his infpection, and bound by fuch rules as he fhall fee fit to impofe. The moft effectual method of obtaining this fecurity is, to veft the fupreme power, civil and ecclefiaftical, in the fame perfon. There is nothing in the nature of temporal power, that renders it unfit to be united with fpiritual : but on the contrary, much mifchief and danger in keeping thefe two branches of power feparate from each other. The magiftrate may poffefs both. The interefts of church and ftate (which are often connected, never oppofite,) may be watched by the fame eye, and guarded by the fame hand. By affuming the particular care of religion, and the fupremacy in religious matters, he is enabled to promote the interefts both of church and ftate in the moft effectual manner."

VI.

VI. *Clergy-maintenance.*

"From the supremacy of the civil magiftrate, is derived the provifion of a legal
maintenance for the minifters of religion.
Were *all* the minifters of religion - placed
in *low* ftations of life, it is eafy to fee, with
what neglect they would be treated, and
with what prejudice their doctrine would
be received. The higheft attainments in
learning and virtue, could never atone for
this one defect (to name no others,) *viz.*
ignorance of what is called the *World.*"

VII. *What fect in religion to be counte-
nanced and fupported by the civil
magiftrate.*

"Where the civil and ecclefiaftical authority are united in a ftate, all the members of the fame commonwealth fhould be
members alfo of the *fame church.* Where
this is impracticable, not the beft, but the
largeft fect will naturally demand the protection of the magiftrate [8]."

VIII. *Submiffion to eftablifhed authority in
church-matters.*

"In this one point the founders of our
holy

holy religion are clear and explicit, that authority once *eftablifhed* muft be obeyed'.— In vain do men unite in religious communities, if each individual is to retain intire liberty of judging and acting for himfelf.— It is not however neceffary, indeed it is not poffible, that even a fmall church-fociety [much lefs a greater] fhould all *agree* in every particular determination. The *fmaller* part therefore muft acquiefce in the judgement of the greater.".

—"Thefe are only the *out-lines* of *church-policy :* to be filled up in different ways, fuited to the infinite varieties of human affairs."

Some general remarks on the foregoing articles.

THERE are fome pofitions interfperfed in them, which are confeffedly juft, and which no men of fober underftanding will ever think of controverting. The fcheme in general is of a worldly caft, and is very well calculated, it muft be owned, to anfwer the ends in view, which feem to be thofe of civil policy only; a fcheme which cannot fail of having many zealous and potent abettors, fo long as their worldly interefts are promoted by it, how much foever

ever

ever the interefts of chriftianity may·fuffer
by fuch an intermixture of human policy
with divine: which is but too vifible in
many inftances. Witnefs the fingle one of
impofing human articles and confeffions
upon the belief and confciences of Chriftians. Which is a manifeft infringement
of Chriftian liberty; a liberty fo plainly
allowed, and fo directly countenanced by·
the Scripture, as well as confirmed by the
voice of reafon.

WHATEVER opinion this gentleman may
have of our eftablifhed articles, or of the
propriety of them to anfwer his purpofe,
he appears to have no very favourable one
of the writers who have pleaded for the
removal of thofe tefts, although they have
given fufficient reafons (and fuch as we
prefume he cannot fairly overthrow) for
the abolifhment of an exaction which does
fo much differvice upon the whole to the
Chriftian caufe. An event which ferious
Chriftians of every denomination, who have
thoroughly ftudied their religion, and difcern the true defign of it, cannot but lament, though they cannot remedy the dif-
order; the powers of this world, in fub-
fervience to their worldly policy, chufing
to keep it ftill on foot, and to continue in
force the laws enacted in favour of it.

SOME

SOME great men of the church, (one at least of the most learned of her prelates) have been " thought to be of opinion, that those who subscribed to the articles, were not obliged to believe them *true*." [If so, by the way, What is the *use* of them? And why is *subscription* to them still required? And what can such subscription after all amount to?——*I subscribe to these articles, not as believing them true;——but——* what?] Now are we to suppose that our archdeacon is one of these non-believing subscribers? I would not myself affirm this; but a writer of note has taken that liberty, speaking out his sentiments without mincing. " I have," saith he, " so good an opinion of Dr. *Balguy's* good sense, notwithstanding the futility of his reasoning in this performance [the consecration sermon] as to think it is a thousand to one, but that he himself is an unbeliever in *many* of those articles ¹⁰."

WITH regard to the *eight* articles above exhibited from that sermon, I may, I hope, with sufficient modesty, declare my own opinion; which is this, that supposing those eight articles were to be established by law, and enjoined to be subscribed by all the clergy, we should soon find many books and

4   pamphlets

pamphlets written on their behalf, explaining, illustrating and commending every one of them, refuting objections, and confirming each article, as usual, with scripture-citations misapplied. Nor can I entertain the least doubt, but the ingenious author of the sermon would appear at the head of the commentators and apologists, being very well qualified to write as large and learned an exposition upon his own, as that celebrated one with which bishop *Burnet* favoured the world on the thirty-nine. His lordship's view in that great attempt, was unquestionably benevolent; being desirous, as far as lay in his power, to alleviate a burthen, which he saw would not in haste be removed from the shoulders of the clergy.

Upon the accidental mention of this great man, who deserved so well from this reverend body, I am inclined to look back a little, and see how they treated him on this very account. With ingratitude enough, for certain, and (which I am sorry to add) with no small degree of ill manners as well as spleen. More particularly, the bigoted part of them in the lower house of convocation, immediately took the alarm, attacked him in form, and mustered up a number of articles against him, which only shewed that their impotence was not inferior

rior

rior to their malevolence. The divines of the old ftamp, addicted to fchoolmen and fyftems, and controverfial theology, were almoft to a man offended with this work; not being able to bear with any fentiments that any way differed from thofe in which they had been educated. The book, they faid, had a dangerous tendency, being full of novel explications, unknown to former churchmen, and abounding with latitudinarian principles, which would infect thofe of the prefent and fucceeding times. Nay, they went fo far as to infinuate, that fome parts of the expofition bordered nearly upon herefy:—*Ut ejus expofitionis caufâ vix* Hærefeos *notam effugerit magni nominis præful,* fays *Welchman.* Which fame *W.* therefore, by the way, takes care not to honour his lordfhip's name with a place in his lift of laudable *authors,* of whom he had availed himfelf in compiling his notes on the articles. Twice indeed he points to a performance of the bifhop, as having been affifted by it, (*viz.* his *Vindication of the ordinations of the church of England,*) but does not once fpecify his name, as being the author of that valuable treatife.—Here the reader may make his own remarks. There feems to be room enough for them.

As

As to the expofition itfelf, archbifhop *Tillotfon*, a very competent judge, gave honourable teftimony to it: and his judgement carried great weight, notwithftanding the cenfure of convocation, and their low artifices to depreciate it. In the prefent age, wherein former prejudices are in good meafure worn off, in comparifon of what they were in thofe days of infatuation, we hear no more of the *herefy* objected to the bifhop; an invention now treated with the contempt it deferves. All fuch of our modern clergy, as have the happinefs not to be attached to the old narrow fyftem, feem to be unanimous in approving the work, and to make the author's fenfe their own in fubfcribing. It is fuppofed, and not without reafon, to be now their general ftandard in that refpect. Yet ftill it is to be wifhed, that they might be tied down to no other ftandard than the *Scripture*. Many objections to their character, occafioned by the prefent injunctions, would hereby be taken off, and greater peace, and more general content, would enfue.—Shall I be pardoned if I afk, What *good* do thefe impofitions do, what *hurt* do they not do, to true chriftianity?

N·

N° II.

Seafonable memento's tendered to Dr. Balguy, on occafion of his uncandid reflections on the authors of fome late writings addreffed to the governors of the church of England.

Cum tua pervideas oculis mala lippus inunctis,
Cur in amicorum vitiis tam cernis acutum
Aut aquila aut ferpens Epidaurius ? At tibi contra
Evenit.——

I. AFTER paffing a favourable cen-fure upon a fet of men, who, as he afferts, " are moft of them out of the reach of rational conviction, and are only to be pitied, not confuted," he is pleafed to add in the fame breath, " There is however *one* clafs of men, to whom this plea for compaffion will not extend : thofe I mean, who, without any pretence to infpiration, live in open war with the national church : with that very church, of which they profefs themfelves minifters, and whofe wages

wages they continue to take, though in actual *service* against her."

THIS paffage has briefly been touched upon before, though judged fcarce to deferve any animadverfions. But however, it may be proper on fome confiderations that have occurred fince, to take a different courfe with the doctor, by reminding him in a gentle manner of fome things, which it may concern him, as well as many other clergymen, to take into fair and ferious confideration.

IF fome of the obfervations intended to be offered, fhall happen to give offence to the learned aggreffor, he will, I hope, fubmit to take the blame to himfelf, recollecting by whom the affault was made:

Sciat
Refponfum non dictum effe, quia læfit prius.

(1) *The plea of compaffion,* it feems, *will not extend to thefe men.* Unhappy mortals! I fhould be forry there fhould be any of the human race, who fhould deferve *no* compaffion; more efpecially fuch men as thofe whom the doctor has here in his eye. He feems to look upon them as a peftilent fet of men, not fit to be trufted with the facred office, nor allowed to continue members

bers of the church; which, he would have us believe, they are not fupporting, but undermining, by the meafures they take. —If therefore upon thefe and the like accounts they deferve no *compaſſion*, are we to fuppofe that in this gentleman's opinion they deferve *puniſhment* ? What puniſhment ſhould that be, and how far ought it to extend ? to bonds and imprifonment ? to the deprivation of livelihood,—or even of life itfelf ? I would hope better things from a mild, a merciful, and well-natured government, fuch as this of *England* is allowed by all to be : Nor, I truſt, will it ever be in the power of uncompaſſionate men, to make it, like themfelves, mercilefs.

(2) *They live in open war with the national church; with that very church, of which they profeſs themfelves miniſters.* Thefe, it muſt be owned, are fevere ſtrokes, but I hope undeferved. For, is it true that they live in open war, or indeed in any war at all, with the church ? By what I have feen, I ſhould think otherwife, and their refpectful applications and requeſts for a review, feem to put the matter out of all doubt. Nor are they enemies to the church, but friends to her, real friends, labouring earneſtly for her good, and ſhewing the greateſt zeal, though tempered with the

C   greateſt

greateſt calmneſs, joined with decency, to
ſerve her true intereſt; and that, without
any gain, or expectation of any, of a temporal nature, for the pains they have taken
to attain this moſt deſireable, but neglected end.

(3.) *They continue to take wages of the
church, though in actual ſervice againſt her.*
—In *ſervice:* As if they were in *pay,* being ſet to work by ſome powerful patrons
and encouragers. A ſuppoſition void of all
probability as well as truth, and not carrying the leaſt appearance of either. Zeal,
honeſt zeal, founded upon much obſervation and reaſon, together with a benevolent wiſh for the advancement of true chriſtianity in this church, appears evidently to
have been the ſole motive which engaged
theſe good men to enter upon this com-
mendable undertaking, and to purſue it
with ſo much ſteadineſs as they have done.

But the gentleman ſpeaks of taking
wages. Does he take none himſelf? Why
then is he offended, and what has he to object to others, that will not in the final
upſhot recoil upon himſelf? He has un-
warily made a ſcourge for his own back;
and ſince he has contrived it for others, it
is fit that he himſelf ſhould, in ſome meaſure,

fure, feel the fmart of it. He fhall therefore be left to the mercy of thofe who well
know how to exercife him to the full, and
will be fure to pay him home in his own coin.

THUS, the bufinefs of *fubfcription* has of
late been matter of much obloquy againft
the clergy, as if they prevaricated in that
act, in order to become intitled to the
bread of the church; to which they have
no other right (it is fuppofed) but either
that of conqueft, or elfe becaufe it is given
them as a reward of iniquity.

I WOULD here take the liberty to afk,
Has our archdeacon never fubfcribed to the
39 articles? If he has, of which I make
no queftion, then I freely affign him over
to the correction of Dr. *Prieftley*; who
fhrewdly gueffes how the matter ftands,
and fcruples not to declare to the world
his apprehenfions about it. Thus he fpeaks:
" I have fo good an opinion of Dr. *Balguy*'s
good fenfe, notwithftanding the futility of
his reafoning in this performance [the *Lambeth*-fermon,] as to think it is a thoufand
to one, but that he himfelf is an unbeliever in many of thofe articles.—Who a-
mong the clergy, that read and think at
all, are fuppofed to believe one third of the
thirty-nine articles of the church of *England?*

land ? "—It might have been expected that a writer, who is fo extremely fevere [as Dr. *B.* is] upon thofe who propofe a reformation in the church, while they continue in it, fhould have expreffed fome degree of indignation againft thofe who intrude themfelves into it by falfe pretences, fubfcribing the articles, *&c.* when they difbelieve and ridicule them.—Men who have come this way into the church, have always proved its firmeft friends, [oppofers of its reformation.] Having made no bones of their own fcruples, they pay no regard to the fcruples of others *."

WHAT will the preacher now fay? Is this fact or not? If it be, he muft in his turn be reminded of his being himfelf included in the fame predicament with the reft of his brethren, and take his fhare with them in the fame condemnation. For he alfo takes *wages* of the church, and continues taking them, in great plenty too, notwithftanding his having in fome refpects forfeited his title to them; efpecially of departing from the original fenfe of any of her articles, or other doctrines, either by preaching, or writing, or both, may juftly

---

* *Confiderations on church-authority,* 1769.

fall

fall under that cenſure. For the original ſenſe, we are told, and it is ſtrongly inſiſted on, is and muſt be the only ſenſe in which we can fairly and honeſtly ſubſcribe. Elſe we render the articles, and ſubſcriptions to them, void and of none effect, and both are good for nothing, —— unleſs for gaining preferment in the church, and acquiring therein the wages of unrighteouſneſs.

WE know the common interrogatories on this occaſion : Why do you take the wages of the church ? Why do you eat her bread ? —Why do you not reſign ? &c.—Theſe are queſtions which ſome men will aſk with great aſſurance, and others will anſwer as they can, when they are pinched.

DR. *B.* may conſider at his leiſure, whe-ther the following reflections may not bear too great a reſemblance to ſome that he knows of, which have been lately thrown out without provocation upon a claſs of men, who are thought to have deſerved better treatment from the aggreſſor : and let the world judge, whether the applica-tion is not much more appoſite in the one caſe, than in the other.——The reflections are tranſcribed from different treatiſes lately publiſhed. Thus the authors ſpeak with-out mincing.

" SOME

" Some put our *articles* on the rack, to find out meanings never meant.—The doctrines of the church are to be learned from the articles and homilies of the church herſelf, not from the private opinions of ſome individuals, who lay hold on the ſkirt of her garment, call themſelves by her name, and live by her revenues."—" Many of the late-born ſons of the church, who live under her roof, and feed themſelves at her table, do not well reliſh her *articles :* And yet they think they may ſafely and conſcientiouſly be ſubſcribed by every individual, who wiſhes to eat the bread of the church, be his religious opinions what they will."—" Who, through baſe and ſelf-intereſted views, ſwear * to doctrines they never believed, and intrude themſelves into the church, in order to ſuck her breaſts, and prey upon her vitals."—" Subtle ſerpents, who lurk within the boſom of the church, only to prey upon her vitals, and who for the ſake of *filthy lucre,* carry on a ſolemn farce of *ſubſcribing* to articles, which many of the ſubſcribers no more believe

---

* I know not what this *ſwearing* may allude to. Does any one *ſwear* to the truth of the articles ?—or of any other doctrines of the church ?

than

than they do mother Goose's tales :—who impiously and hypocritically set their hands to doctrines, which in their hearts they never assented to," &c.

THESE are free reflections indeed. Does Dr. *B*. approve of them ? I will venture to say, he does not. And yet, upon his anti-reforming principles, our articles must never be altered, nor subscriptions to them ever be dismissed out of the church. Consequently, these and the like reflections will always continue to be flung out against the clergy, as perverting the sense of the church, into a sense of their own, and introducing into it a new sort of divinity, which the reformers of it never dreamed of. What an hardship is this, brought upon the clergy in an age of ignorance, and continued upon them in an age of knowledge! And yet, those who endeavour to rid them of such a burden, receive but little thanks, and, what is more, are charged with being in actual service against the church (can you believe it ?) for their so doing. A little more civility, a little more consistency in the opposers, would tend more to their credit, as well as to the benefit of the church of *England*.

C 4   II.

II. THE archdeacon, I think, has done
no great credit either to himſelf, or to his
political church, when he comes to touch
upon the ſubject of excommunication, and
deprivation. It is ſomewhat unhappy that
this gentleman is ſo often making a rod for
his own chaſtiſement, when he is contriving and intending it for the chaſtiſement
of others, Not aware, we may ſuppoſe,
of the conſequences, nor probably fore-
ſeeing how far men will carry on the hint
which he unwittingly throws in their way,
he renders himſelf liable to many attacks
at law, which, notwithſtanding his dignity, would give him much trouble, and
probably coſt him much money, if others
ſhould be inclined to be as ſevere upon
him, as he ſeems willing to be upon them.
Whoever narrowly looks into our laws,
examines and conſiders well our rubrics
and canons, and other ſtrict injunctions of
church and ſtate, in regard to the office
and duties of the clergy, will find that
they are not only very numerous, but at
the ſame time many of them very difficult
to be performed, eſpecially with that puncti-
lious exactneſs, with which ſome men
would inſiſt it is neceſſary to perform them,
Shew me a clergyman in all *England* that

can

can truly fay, laying his hand upon his breaft, " All thefe laws, ordinances, injunctions, rules, rubrics and canons, have I kept, and punctually obferved, in all my conduct, ever fince I have been in holy orders : I defy any man in *England* to charge me with any the leaft default, deviation, or tranfgreffion in fuch matters, and to prove them againft me, in any court, civil or ecclefiaftical, within his Majefty's dominions." Who, or where is the man, among the clergy of thefe realms, that can make this open and bold appeal ? If there be any fuch man, he may well deferve, at the next vacancy, to fucceed in the archdeaconry of Winchefter. Mean while, it is well for the clergy, that the common people (who, notwithftanding the good inftructions perpetually given them, are, many of them, very litigious,) do not know the hundredth part of the niceties of the laws refpecting the facred order. Neverthelefs, fome bold man may arife hereafter, who may think it worth his while, to exhibit to the public view, a large catalogue of articles (much larger than thofe commonly iffued out from the ecclefiaftical courts) upon which the church-wardens from thence forward may form their prefentments, and thereby experimentally prove to bufy meddlers,

dlers, that it is not fafe meddling with edged
tools, and that fome mens weapons may
happen in the end to be turned againft
themfelves, by thofe, who can manage them
more dextroufly, and with greater force.

N° III.

Concurring sentiments of several learn-
ed and judicious persons concerning
the right of private judgement in
matters of religion.

THE sentiments of Dr. *Balguy* on this
head, have been seen already, and
been also in part considered. In an age of
so much good sense and free inquiry, one
would have little expected to see the cause
of liberty discountenanced, or rendered dubious, by a person of so much understanding and learning as the doctor; who might
well have been supposed to entertain more
liberal sentiments on the subject, and more
friendly to the community. We may still
hope, that he cannot have many abettors in
this particular, among men of thought and
examination. It may be proper to exhibit
here some few out of many solid and just
observations, made by several able divines,
expressing a different judgement from his
on the present argument.

1. THE

1. THE late learned and refpectable Dr. *Berriman*, every one knows, was a ftaunch friend to our conftitution in church and ftate ;—and at the fame time, no enemy to the exertion of the fecular power in matters ecclefiaftical. Speaking of the exercife of private judgement on religious fubjects, he makes thefe free and juft conceffions. "The truth is, all men are obliged to confider ferioufly, and ufe all proper methods to inform their *judgement*, as to matters of religion. After this, the conviction of their judgement will become to them a rule of action, and direct them in their refpective ftations and offices of life." *Sermon on the authority of the civil powers in matters of religion*, 1722. And he fpeaks very well to the fame purpofe, giving a proper caution, in another difcourfe.— "Though the ufe of private judgement be neceffary, yet the teachings of a private fpirit may be dangerous. And therefore, as I would require no man to believe implicitly, but advife every one to *judge for himfelf*, in proportion to the reach of his abilities ; fo at the fame time it is fit he be reminded to call in all proper help and affiftance to direct his judgement." *Sermon to the religious focieties*, 1739.

2. ANO-

2. ANOTHER divine of note for contro-versial divinity, and well esteemed by a late metropolitan for his abilities in that way, expresses himself with equal justice and propriety in favour of the rights of private judgement.

" THE right of the church to determine for her members, does not exclude the rights of *private judgement.* The church hath a right of determining, so far only as she determines *agreeable to the word of God*[12]. These rights coincide, and are in effect but one and the same thing; though always with this difference, that the judgement of society[13] is a judgement of authority, while private judgement is no more than a judgement of discretion or opinion[14]. This latter cannot be excluded by the decisions of any authority upon earth: for thoughts are free; and if they are absurd or injurious, they must be accounted for at last to the searcher of all hearts."—But then, as " such private judgement, he justly observes, will not be *authoritative* or binding to *others;* so, he no less freely acknowledges, the authority of the church in matters of religion, is and must be circumscribed within proper limits." For instance : " We all grant, says he, that the legislative

power

power of the church cannot extend to matters of *doctrine:* which power can reach only to forms and circumſtantials, and matters of diſcipline [1] ; but *doctrines* reſt wholly upon the power of God, and the authority of divine revelation." *Remarks on the principles and ſpirit of the* Confeſſional, *by the Rev.* W. Jones,—*rector of* Pluckley *in* Kent, 1770, p. 24, 25, 103.

[This occaſional mention of *church-authority* (which ſome zealots have carried to an enormous height, in oppoſition to the claims of *private judgement)* brings opportunely into my mind, the account given by archbiſhop *Synge* of *Daniel Herly,* a poor *Iriſh* peaſant ; which I ſuppoſe will gratify the reader's curioſity, and furniſh him with many uſeful reflections on theſe two articles.

" *Daniel,* his grace tells us, was naturally very inquiſitive after knowledge of all ſorts, as he had opportunity for it : but, above all, he was moſt carefully attentive to thoſe rational arguments, which by men of all religions are brought to prove the certainty of a life to come, &c. ' Since God,' ſaid he, in one of his conferences with a Romiſh prieſt, who would have diſſuaded him from turning proteſtant,—

5   ' has

' has given me some degree of reason and understanding, I think myself obliged to make the best *inquiry* I can into the way of salvation ; and if, for want of such inquiry, I should run the hazard of being misled, I cannot but think, that God would punish me for my negligence.—I shall endeavour to make the best use I can of my *bible* ; and as for those passages in it, which are doubtful and difficult, I shall not take upon me to interpret them ; nor will I offer to form any opinion from such passages as are obscure, except they are plainly cleared up to my satisfaction."

BEING, at another time, pressed by the priest with the *authority of the church* (meaning that of *Rome,*) " Sir, says *Daniel,* I gather my faith and religion altogether from such passages of *scripture* as are very plain : and these plain passages enable me to understand many more, which otherwise, perhaps, would be obscure and doubtful. I am answerable to *God,* and to none but him, for my honesty and sincerity in this way of proceeding. But I do not see what *authority* any *church* has to impose Her *interpretations* upon Me, when my clearest understanding assures me that these same interpretations are contrary to the plain meaning of the *scripture* itself, and some of them to common

mon

mon fenſe and reaſon. I deſire you to prove, if you can, that God has given ſuch au-thority as you maintain, to any, and what church; and to ſhew me who it is that is, by God's appointment, to inform me of the true meaning of the church's *interpreta-tions*, in caſe that I do not at firſt under-ſtand them.——It is abſolutely impoſſible for me to believe any doctrine before I am convinced of the truth of it, either by the reaſon of the thing itſelf, or by the *divine authority* of him that teaches it. Matters of *fact* I can and do believe upon the teſtimony of credible witneſſes: but bare *authority*, excepting that of God himſelf, cannot poſ-ſibly bring me to the belief of any *religious doctrine.*"

SHALL I here tell you how the conference ended? Our author goes on to acquaint us, that the prieſt, not being able to give a *ra-tional* anſwer to what *Daniel* had thus urged, betook himſelf to another way, that is very common among them; and, with great aſ-ſurance told him, that he would certainly be *damned* if he became a *proteſtant*. But ſays *Daniel*, "*Who art thou that judgeſt ano-ther's ſervant? To his own maſter he ſtandeth or falleth: yea, he ſhall be holden up: for God is able to make him ſtand. Rom. xiv. 4.*" Very well ſpoken for certain. Here is good plain

plain fenfe and honefty on the one hand;
and only groundlefs menace, and, in effect,
giving up the caufe, for want of argument,
on the other. And who of all the Romifh
priefts, with all their fubtlety, could have
invalidated the folid arguments upon which
Daniel maintained his converfion, and the
caufe of Proteftantifm ?—Dr. *Balguy* may
now reflect, if he pleafes, upon the "attempt
of this poor *Daniel* to exercife his feeble underftanding, in judging for himfelf" in matters of religion; and may alfo, if he fhall
think proper, call this piece of conduct,
" the caprice and folly of a difordered imagination." But will he, at the fame time,
have the affurance to add, that *Daniel* was
" embarraffed by the fpecious and plaufible
arguments" of the Romifh prieft ?

THIS little narrative may feem to be a
fort of digreffion, but co-incides exactly
with the main fubject I am upon : to the
purfuit of which I now proceed.]

3. " WE cannot, if we would, conform
our faith to the dictates of *another*, and believe juft as he believes, and becaufe he believes fo : nor can it ever poffibly be lawful, upon any account, to comply with, or
agree to any thing in religion that is contrary to our judgement, and the inward per-

D   fuafion

suasion of our minds; to profess for truth, what we believe to be a wrong faith, or false doctrine; and to worship God after any other manner, than that which we conceive to be most agreeable to the divine will. In these matters we can neither give, nor can another usurp, any authority over our consciences; nor can we submit them to any other ruler, but God and our own reason." Dr. *Ibbot*'s sermon before the Lord Mayor, *Sept.* 29, 1720.

4. " THE true knowledge of religion naturally leads men to a *rational* belief of it; which should equally be the object of our zealous concern.—The great truths of the gospel are to be learnt from the *word of God.*—We ought not only to search and study the scriptures ourselves, but to stir up others to study them, with an unwearied zeal, a steady attention, and a hearty love of the *truth* :—And after proving and *examining* all things, we ought to hold fast that which we find to be good and true: neither blindly submitting our judgement to human authority, nor making our own opinion the standard of that of other men. In fine, we should earnestly contend for that faith, and form of sound doctrine, which was once for all delivered to the *first* Christians; and endeavour to preserve it in its
ancient

ancient purity and fimplicity; by diftinguifhing the genuine doctrine of Chrift
and his apoftles, from the *traditionary en-
largements,* with which, in every age, it
haf been more or lefs clogged and blend-
ed. —— " Others have the fame right to
differ from Us, that we have to differ from
Them.—If we treat others ill for profeffing what is the refult of their diligent and
honeft inquiries into the will of God, we
fet up our own judgement as the ftandard
of revealed truth; and would oblige others
to believe only fuch things as We determine and enjoin, without allowing them
the liberty to *judge for themfelves.* This is
a moft unrighteous encroachment upon the
common privilege of mankind : For, to *inquire freely* into the truth of every thing
that is propofed to us for our belief or our
practice, is the natural and unalienable right
of every man : it is the indifpenfable duty
of every Chriftian : it is the characteriftic of
a true Proteftant : it is the joy and triumph
of every true *Briton.* It is a right that we
can fcarce over-value : and which we cannot give up, without renouncing the chief
ufe of our reafon ; which is the glory of our
nature ; and was given us to be the guide
of all our actions; but more efpecially of
our moral and religious conduct. Without

this

this *freedom of inquiry*, there can be no rational belief, no fincere practice of religion and virtue : but inftead of a reafonable faith, credulity muft prevail ; and hypocrify inftead of devotion : religion would degenerate into fuperftition, and a Chriftian zeal be turned into bitter rage, and cruel bigotry.

" Let us therefore beware of difcouraging that *liberty of inquiry*, and of *private judgement*, which is the fundamental principle of our *reformation*, and the only firm fupport of all true religion. And though we cannot always avoid differing in our opinions, when we really *judge for ourfelves*, let us however treat one another with juftice, and candour, and a friendly refpect. This fair ufage is due to all perfons, whatever their perfuafions may be : and is far more apt to gain upon their minds, to reclaim them from error, or to reform their practice, than the more common methods, *&c.*" Dr. *Stevenfon*'s ferm. at the bifhop of *Hereford*'s vifitation, 1728.

5. " Prove all things. All who have the ufe of their reafon, are obliged by this precept, to examine and judge for themfelves, upon the beft information they can get, and in the proper ufe of the helps and

and advantages that are afforded them, that they may be fully perfuaded in their own minds, and be able to give a reafon unto others of the hope that is in them.

" This precept is founded in the very nature and reafon of things : for, unlefs every Chriftian be allowed to examine and judge for himfelf of what he is to believe and practife, there can be no fuch thing as true faith, nor confequently any religion. Now faith is a rational perfuafion of the truth of things not feen ; which neceffarily implies the exercife of our faculties, and the ufe of our reafon ; nor is it poffible for us, any other way, to arrive at a well-grounded faith, or at a rational and virtuous practice. And therefore, whatever principles of religion we embrace, if they are not the refult of a free, honeft, and impartial inquiry, and the matter of our deliberate choice, they muft be looked upon as vain and ground-lefs, and neither acceptable to God, nor truly fatisfactory to our own minds.

" This right of private judgement is infeparably connected with the fuppofition of our being *rational*; and our obligation to the exercife of it, arifeth from the very frame and conftitution of human nature.

" Can

" Can it be imagined, that the all-wife and beneficent author of our beings would have endowed all men with reafon, underftanding, and liberty, if he had not intended that all men fhould equally exercife them, and more efpecially fo in the examination and choice of their religious principles ?——Either therefore we muft admit, that they are to judge for themfelves, and to take up with fuch fentiments in religion as, upon due examination, fhall appear to them to be right, and receive the approbation of their reafon and confcience: or elfe we muft fuppofe, that thofe noble powers and faculties, which do fo eminently diftinguifh them from inferior beings, and on the right ufe whereof their fupreme perfection and happinefs depend, are, in great meafure, infignificant and trifling, nay, altogether impertinent and ufelefs, as to the chief and only valuable end of their exiftence."

Hence it appears that " no man whatfoever, nor any body of men, can lawfully claim any authority over the confciences and judgements of other men, nor require an implicit fubmiffion to their fentiments of things, though in themfelves true and worthy of acceptation: for in this refpect all men are upon a level, and have an equal
right

right to exercife their faculties, and determine their judgements by the evidence that
appears to them.

" Upon the whole, we muft fee with
our own eyes, and perceive with our own
underftandings, and not take our religion
upon truft, and regulate our faith and practice, either by the traditions of our anceftors, or by the mere dictates of our fpiritual guides and inftructors. And though
in fome cafes there is a regard to be paid to
antiquity, and what has been held and
practifed in the church for many fucceffive
generations, may challenge a candid and decent treatment; yet our affent and compliance muft arife from the conviction of our
minds, and be built upon more rational
grounds, than either the venerable name of
antiquity, or the authority and examples of
great and worthy men.

" This duty of exercifing our right of
private judgement, is ftrongly enforced by
the holy fcripture. Our bleffed Saviour refers us to the facred records for the credentials
of his miffion, and the truth of his doctrines. *Search the fcriptures*, faith he : And,
*Be not ye called Rabbi, neither be ye called
Mafters ; for one is your mafter, even Chrift.*
And St. *Paul* exhorteth Chriftians to exa-

mine

mine the grounds of their religion, and to embrace it only upon conviction and choice. *I speak as unto wise men; judge ye what I say.* — *Prove all things; hold fast that which is good.* And St. *John; Believe not every spirit, but try the spirits, whether they be of God.*

" WE also find a very high commendation bestowed upon the conduct of the *Bereans,* who received not even the doctrines of the inspired apostles, till they had first searched the scriptures, to see whether those things were so or not. And so the church of *Ephesus,* in the Revelation, is honoured with the approbation of Christ himself, for having *examined* the pretences of those who said they were apostles, but were not, and found them liars.

" UPON this principle the *reformation* was at first founded, and doth still subsist: If we give it up, we shall sap the foundation, and the superstructure will soon fall to the ground."

THE general inference and conclusion is this.

" THIS right of private judgement *which has been asserted,* lays a foundation for mutual
tual

tual charity and forbearance, notwithstanding our differences of opinion; provided
they neither prejudice the cause of virtue,
nor entrench upon the peace of society. In
this imperfect state, it is not to be expected that all men should think exactly alike;
nor doth it appear to have been ever intended by the wise author of our beings.——
Since therefore there is no way of preventing all variety of sentiments in religion,
without destroying the order of nature, and
quite altering the present frame and consti-
tution of things; we should be content to
enjoy our own sentiments, without denying
the same privilege to others, who as Men
and Christians have an equal right to it."
Mr. *Myonnet's* Sermon before the Lord
Mayor at St. *Paul's*, 5 *Nov.* 1736.

AFTER such good authorities produced
in proof of the right of private judgement,
one might now venture to ask Dr. *Balguy*,
what he thinks of them, and whether he
supposes himself able to demolish them, by
arguments of greater force, of his own
framing?—To the foregoing I could sub-
join the authorities of *Chillingworth, Locke,*
and several other writers of eminent abilities, whose arguments in the behalf of liberty could never yet be answered, to the
satisfaction of competent judges, by any
that

that oppofed them. But I forbear for the prefent, and would afk the doctor next, whether he can have affurance enough to oppofe his opinion on this argument, to the more liberal and united fentiments of his fuperiors in the church, to whofe judgement in fuch matters, according to his own avowed principles, the greateft deference is due. The following prelates, of great name and merit, do each of them fpeak home to the purpofe.

6. " No one can have a *faith* of his own, who makes not ufe of his *own judgement,* in fixing in his mind what God calls upon him to believe, as neceffary to a Chriftian.— Without this, he will be fo far from contending for the faith once delivered to the faints, that he cannot know fo much as what that faith is, nor have any faith at all to contend for.—In order to find out the faith once delivered, we muft all endeavour, to the utmoft of our power, to find out the true fenfe of thofe paffages in which any thing is declared neceffary to be believed in order to our falvation ; and to this purpofe, muft make ufe of our *own underftandings,* and form the beft judgement we ourfelves can."—Again : " As it is abfurd to fuppofe, that any man can be faved by the faith of another ; or by any belief, but what

what is truly his own : fo there is no poffible method of having a faith of his own,
properly fo called, without building it entirely upon what appears right to his own
judgement, fuch as it is, after his beft endeavours for information." Bp. *Hoadly*'s
difc. on *Jude* 3.

7. " As we enjoy the bleffing of *liberty*
in that perfection, which has been unknown
to former ages, and is fo ftill to moft other
nations; let us be diligent in ufing it to
the good purpofes for which it is fo libe-
rally indulged us; and render ours as much
fuperior to thofe nations that are yet deprived of it, as moft other countries are
obferved to have been in the like circumftances. Let us concur with this aufpicious
courfe of Providence, and each contribute
our endeavours towards carrying on this
progrefs (of religion,) by every ferious, fair,
and *free inquiry*; free, not only from all
outward violence and clamour, but alfo
from all inward bitternefs, wrath, and ha-
tred : learning to bear with one another's
miftakes, and labouring as well to reform
the errors of our brethren in love, as to
promote and confirm their knowledge of
the truth ; *not for that*, in either cafe, *we
have dominion over their faith*; *but as being
helpers of their joy.* And thus fhall religion
be

be at length fuffered to partake the benefit
of thofe *improvements,* which every thing
befide enjoys." Bp. *Law's* confiderations
on the theory of religion (ed. 1765) p.
260, &c.

8. " WE ought to promote and to en-
courage the advancement of religious knowledge, and the only means by which it can
be advanced, *freedom of inquiry.*—Chriftianity has always flourifhed or decayed together with learning and liberty : it will ever
ftand or fall with them. It is therefore of
the utmoft importance to the caufe of true
religion, that it be fubmitted to an open
and impartial *examination ;* that every *dif-
quifition* concerning it be allowed its free
courfe ; that even the malice of its enemies
fhould have its full fcope, and try it's utmoft ftrength of argument againft it.—
What has been the confequence of all that
licentious contradiction, with which the
gofpel has been received in thefe our times,
and in this nation? Has it not given birth
to fuch irrefragable apologies and convinc-
ing illuftrations of our moft holy religion,
as no other age or nation ever produced ?—
Let no one lightly entertain fufpicions of
any ferious propofal for the advancement
of religious knowledge; nor out of unreafonable prejudice endeavour to obftruct
any

any *inquiry* that profeſſes to aim at the
farther illuſtration of the great ſcheme of
the goſpel in general, or the removal of
error in any part, in faith, in doctrine, in
practice, or in worſhip. An opinion is
not therefore falſe becauſe it contradicts received notions : but whether true or falſe,
let it be ſubmitted to a *fair examination :*
truth muſt in the end be a gainer by it, and
appear with the greater evidence. Where
freedom of inquiry is maintained and exer-
ciſed under the direction of the ſincere *word
of God,* falſhood may perhaps triumph for
a day, but to-morrow truth will certainly
prevail, and every ſucceeding day will confirm her ſuperiority.—By the bleſſing of
God upon the free exerciſe of *reaſon* and
private judgement, the labours of the learned have been greatly ſucceſsful in promot-
ing religious knowledge." Dr. *Lowth's*
viſitation-ſermon at *Durham,* 1758. And
this right reverend and worthy perſonage
ſpeaks to the ſame purpoſe (in favour of the
liberty of private judgement) in the aſſize-
ſermon which he preached there. " Our
religious eſtabliſhment, ſaith his lordſhip, is
founded on the right of *private judgement ;*
and freely allows to others, that liberty
which it hath vindicated to itſelf."

9. Another learned prelate, who ſtudied
this

this fubject with great attention, and was fufficiently cautious not to allow too much fcope to religious liberty, and the exercife of private judgement, freely and readily makes the following conceffions in their favour, which have done him honour, and rendered his tracts more valuable, *viz.* " Every man muft have a right to judge finally for himfelf in all matters of religion."—" All Chriftians fhould duly exercife, and be finally determined by, their own judgement, refpectively, as to all matters of faith and practice in religion."— " From the exprefs and repeated declarations of the Scriptures of the New Teftament, it is evident, that God intended to give to every one a right to judge, at all times ultimately for himfelf, in all matters of religion." Bp. *Ellis's* tracts on liberty, 1767. p. 17, 19, 35.

ALL thefe weighty authorities in fupport of the right of private judgement, may now feem abundantly fufficient to bear down the objections of Dr. *B.* who hath endeavoured to leffen our efteem for this valuable privilege, in order thereby to give the greater folidity to his own fcheme.

THERE is however one mafterly (tho' anonymous) author remaining, who hath lately

lately written with great fpirit and clear-
nefs as well as ftrength of argument, on this
fubject, and feems to have given the con-
cluding ftroke to all that can well be faid
upon it. I cannot therefore difmifs this
collection of authorities, to my fatisfaction,
without fubjoining to them the following
remarks of this able and engaging writer.

10. " THE religion of Jefus utterly dif-
claims all dominion over the faith and confcience of men. We are exprefsly forbidden
by our Lord himfelf, to acknowledge any authority in points of faith and religion befides his : and are exprefsly told that in
things of this nature we are all brethren,
having an equal power and authority over
each other, i. e. in truth, none at all : *One
is our mafter, even Chrift.*

" IN our inquiring after truth, we fhould
carefully lay afide all prejudice and prepof-
feffion, in favour of any theological notions
or opinions that we may have haftily taken
up, through the dint of cuftom and education, or through an implicit and blind
fubmiffion to the canons and injunctions of
men.

" IT is an idle and imaginary thing to
fuppofe that infallibility fhould be lodged in

4   one

one man, or be the peculiar diftinguifhing privilege of any one church. I muft after all *judge for myfelf*; fince no man in matters of religion and confcience has any more right to judge and determine for me in this world, than he has to fit in judgement upon me hereafter.——If I am anfwerable for the ufe and exercife of my underftanding, why fhould I refign it to another? Or how, or with what face, can any fober and reafonable perfon infift upon it?——My right of thinking and judging for myfelf, will difturb no man's peace, whilft I allow him as freely to exercife the fame right.

" Many have weakly contended for the neceffity of a perfect uniformity and agreement in articles of faith, and urged their own creeds and canons as the only ftandards of truth and orthodoxy, when it is too plain and evident to be denied that fuch an exact and perfect uniformity is not to be expected, nor is it any where to be found, not even in the church of *Rome* herfelf, notwithftanding all her loud boafts of infallibility.——If we are Proteftants upon principle, why fhould we take any doctrines for granted, upon the bare affertion, the credit or authority of others, or becaufe we have received them from our anceftors? Or what good reafon can be affigned why we
fhould

fhould not reject the miftakes of our fore-
fathers, as they rejected thofe of the church
of *Rome?*——The caufe in which we are
all profeffedly embarked as proteftants,
feems to reft entirely upon the exercife of
private judgement, and the right which
every man has to the free ufe of the holy
fcriptures; and I am perfuaded, that a general and ftrict adherence to this truly proteftant principle, had we room to hope for
it, would tend more than any thing elfe, to
fap the foundations, and fhake the whole
fyftem of popery.——And how indeed can
we expect that farther reformation, which
is by many fo much defired and wifhed for,
unlefs, as proteftants, we uniformly purfue,
and fteadily act upon the fame principle?
Upon this principle our feparation from the
church of *Rome* is fully juftified, and [upon
this] we might hope to fee Chriftian liberty
and truth, and real religion, gain yet more
ground. *Effay on the right of private judgement, prefixed to a Work entitled,* The True
Doctrine of the New Teftament concerning
Jefus Chrift confidered, p. 14, 9, 47, 25,
30, 33, 34.

THE ingenious author of this effay
pleads the caufe of this invaluable right fo
well, and argues in its favour upon fuch
clear and folid principles, that I believe every
candid and benevolent reader, and friend to

E   liberty,

liberty, will be well pleafed if I prefent him with a farther view of the writer's thoughts on this head.

. " No man can plead an exclufive privilege, or have any better plea than another, for infifting upon a right to judge and determine for another; but every one has an indifputable right to judge for himfelf: every honeft and confcientious man will do it; every true proteftant will look upon the *fcripture* as his fafeft and fureft guide in doing it; and every fincere lover of truth, every meek and humble Chriftian, may hope for, and reckon upon fuch affiftance of the Spirit of God, as will enable him by this rule to judge and determine for himfelf, in all controverfies of religion, as far as is needful, or néceffary, in order to his acceptance with God, and his final happinefs. One private Chriftian hath certainly as good authority and right to fearch the fcriptures, and judge of truth and falfhood, as another. If he has a capacity for it, as is here fuppofed, he certainly has a right to do it, a right that no man can juftly deprive him of. And, for any church to deny or refufe him this juft and rightful claim, is what directly tends to deftroy all religion and virtue. For what is religion or faith without underftanding ? Or what is virtue

4   or

or morality without reafon, liberty, and freedom of choice ?——

" For any one to fet up himfelf as an *authorifed interpreter* of fcripture, fo as to pafs his own interpretations for laws, and demand from others an implicit faith and blind fubmiffion, is going greater lengths than what our Saviour himfelf, or his apoftles after him, ever did, or gave any the leaft countenance for doing.—If the fcriptures, which were indited by an infallible fpirit, are a more fure rule than any interpretations of fallible men, as they certainly are, why muft I *fubfcribe* to the words *which man's wifdom teacheth*, and not acquiefce in the words *which the holy* gofpel *teacheth ?* Or why fhould any force be put upon the underftanding, any violence offered to the confcience of Men, who cannot believe as they pleafe, and who dare not lie in profeffing to believe what they do not ? Sure I am, that no other methods but thofe of argument, reafon, and evidence, can poffibly be of any effect in the difputable and lefs neceffary points of religion.——

" Let thofe whom it more immediately concerns ferioufly reflect, whether they can fairly fupport and vindicate any fuch meafures, as can only tend to blind and fhackle the

the human underſtanding, and put a ſtop
to that freedom of ſentiment and inquiry,
which is the *natural right* of every man, in
a peculiar ſenſe the birth-right and glory of
every true *proteſtant*, who, if he rightly
underſtands himſelf, and his own principles,
will never be hurried away with the authority of great names, whether ancient or
modern, nor biaſſed by education, cuſtom,
or intereſt, as is too much the manner and
way of the world." p. 24, 25, 26, 18, 19.

I cannot better cloſe up theſe notes, aſſert-
ing the right of private judgement, than by
recommending the fine obſervations following, whereby the author would engage
Chriſtians to mutual forbearance, and unity
of ſpirit, in the midſt of their different ſentiments about religion, or any external
modes and circumſtances annexed to it.
To *forbear one another in love*, is an apoſto-
lical injunction ; and the conſtant exerciſe
of it, amongſt all denominations, would
tend very much to the peace and happineſs
of the Chriſtian world.

" SOME differences in principle, opinion,
and ſentiment, will always ſubſiſt in all
communities. Summaries of faith are no
ſure guard againſt them. Nor is it at all to
be wondered at, that men ſhould form a
different

different opinion and judgement, as in other things, so in their interpretation and sense of the sacred writings. Nay, the inspired writers themselves do every where take it for granted, that Christians will differ as to their *judgement* in many things. They may *think* differently, and yet *walk* by the *same rule*: or they may, notwithstanding some difference in *opinion* or persuasion, be at *unity* with one another, having the *same love*, being of *one accord*, of *one mind*. Their *religion* will teach them humanity, forbearance, and good-nature one towards another. True piety and charity will always perfectly harmonize and unite. And the great principles of Christianity, rightly understood, will strengthen and perfect that union which ought to subsist in every religious and civil society. We are therefore exhorted as Christians, to keep, — not an unity of *opinion* in the bond of *ignorance*, nor an unity of *profession* in the bond of *hypocrisy*, but an unity of *spirit* in the bond of *peace*. And herein it is [herein alone] that true *Christian unity* does consist: not so much in uniformity of opinion, as in unanimity of affection, in love and peace, in mutual charity and good-will, and in all kind and friendly offices, as it becometh brethren in Christ Jesus; who all hold the same head, and acknowledge one and the same Lord,

and

and who are (as to every thing material or neceſſary,) of the ſame mind and judgement [and of the ſame univerſal church of Chriſt,] however denominated or diſtinguiſhed in other reſpects." p. 15, 16.———

AGAIN, " A diverſity of opinions there is, and always will be, among Chriſtians, even proteſtants of every denomination, and thoſe of the very ſame religious ſociety. So long as men are of one mind in the greateſt articles (ſuch as the belief of a God, his providence, a future ſtate, a judgement to come, the divine authority of the ſcriptures, the neceſ-, ſity of a godly life, and its acceptableneſs with God to ſalvation, through Jeſus Chriſt,) there is no need of being of one mind, as to other matters. Nay, ſo long as good men agree to differ, and carry on their inquiries and debates with a Chriſtian temper and ſpirit, this is ſo far from being injurious to the peace of the community, that the church and the world may be greatly edified and improved by it; light and knowledge will increaſe, and truth be the more likely to ſpread and prevail." *ibid.* p. 30, 31.

WHAT the eſſayiſt notes above concerning uniformity of opinion, and the little avail of it in compariſon of the exerciſe of the Chriſtian temper, is truly amiable, and may

may well be applied to all other inftances of ecclefiaftical uniformity. I have the plea-fure to obferve, that the learned Dr. *Moore* expreffes the fame fentiments, with regard to thefe fuppofed marks of orthodoxy and conformity. " A mutual agreement of bearing with one another's diffents in the *non-fundamentals* of religion, is really a greater ornament of Chriftianity, than the moft exact *uniformity* imaginable; it being an eminent act or exercife of Chriftian *charity*, (the flower of all Chriftian graces,) and the beft way, I think, at the long run, to make the *church* as *uniform*, as can juftly be defired." *Preface to m. of godlin.* p. 17.

N°

Some specimens of the learning and other qualifications of our principal reformers, for drawing up articles of theology, to be the standard of the doctrines of the church of England.

OUR reformers, to their juſt praiſe be it ſpoken, were excellent men, and their names ought for ever to be had in honourable remembrance by all *Britiſh* proteſtants. To them, under God, we owe one of the greateſt of bleſſings, the recovering of our Chriſtian liberty from the vaſſalage of popery, and arbitrary ſway over our reaſon and our conſciences, and alſo, in many caſes, over our lives and fortunes. Our good, our great and glorious deliverers, paſſed through innumerable, and almoſt inſuperable difficulties, in order to regain to us theſe invaluable benefits, and at laſt, on that account, gave up their lives, and all that was dear to them in this world, as a ſacrifice in the

the caufe of truth ; expiring in the greateft
tortures that their inhuman adverfaries
could invent, to put a ftop to their farther
progrefs in reforming.

IT is evident from hiftory, that they
would have gone much farther than they
did in the reformation they intended, if
the times had been more favourable. But
thanks be to almighty God, that they were
permitted and enabled to do fo much as
they have done for us. They laid the foundation, leaving the fuperftructure to be
carried on and compleated by their fucceffors.

ONE other, and no fmall difadvantage
which they unhappily laboured under, and
which from their time to this, has been
matter of juft regret to true friends to divine
revelation, was their defect of knowledge
in facred matters, above all, in the true fenfe
of Scripture. Critical learning therein was
at that time at a low ebb : nor could it well
be otherwife, confidering the abyfs of ignorance and fuperftition in which they had
been long immerfed, and out of which they
were then gradually emerging. I have numerous inftances in my view, to prove the
truth of this affertion ; but for the prefent, I pafs them over, contenting myfelf,

as

as I hope I shall my readers, with a few specimens.

In the first edition of our *English* liturgy, 1548, they retained the old *exorcising* form in the office of baptizing infants. Ridiculous enough for certain, as it may now appear to Us, but it did not, it seems, appear so to Them, in those less enlightened days. Here it follows.

" *Then let the priest, looking upon the children, say,* I command thee, unclean spirit ", in the name of the Father, of the Son, and of the Holy Ghost, that thou come out and depart from these infants, whom our Lord Jesus Christ hath vouchsafed to call to his holy baptism, to be made members of his body, and of his holy congregation. Therefore, thou cursed spirit, remember thy sentence, remember thy judgement, remember the day to be at hand, wherein thou shalt burn in fire everlasting, prepared for thee and thy angels. And presume not hereafter to exercise thy tyranny towards these infants *, whom Christ hath bought with

---

* As to the origin of this custom of exorcising, it seems to have been applied at first to *adults* only, not to infants. " In the ancient ages of the church, says Mr. *Wheatly,* a custom obtained to cast the devil out of the person baptized,

with his precious blood, and by his holy
baptifm calleth to be of his flock."

SOME other very exceptionable paffages
may be feen here and there in our old com-
mon-prayer books, particularly the firft,
which neverthelefs fome modern proteftants
(Dr. *Hickes,* if I remember right, for one)
have not fcrupled to extol as the beft and
moft primitive form of public fervice we
ever had in our language.

---

tized, who was fuppofed to have taken poffeffion of the
catechumen in his unregenerate ftate." How then came
this folemn farce to be acted in the cafe of young *infants?*
And is the latter part of the 72d canon (which is ftill in
force) now put in practice?——The fame author takes notice of another abfurdity, in which our reformers were unhappily involved at that time ; having a notion, a ftrange
one it was, that in fome cafes baptifm muft at all events be
performed, though in private, though in the greateft
hurry, and many times by any layman or woman prefent,
rather than that the infant fhould die unbaptized, or, in the
phrafe of an unbeliever, be left in the *paws of the roaring
lion.* This notion and practice, Mr. *Wheatly* tells us, was
founded upon an error which our reformers had imbibed in
the Romifh church, concerning the impoffibility of falvation without the facrament of baptifm : which therefore,
being in their opinions fo abfolutely neceffary, they chofe
fhould be adminiftered by any body that was prefent, in
cafes of extremity, rather than any fhould die without it.
But afterwards they came to have clearer notions of the facraments, and perceived how abfurd it was to confine the
mercies of God to outward means. And yet even ftill we
find the rubric fpeaking of *great caufe* and *neceffity,* of *need
compelling,* &c.

If

IF we would next form our judgement of the abilities of our reformers to frame for us a fyftem of doctrines which fhould remain a perpetual ftandard of belief and profeffion in the *Englifh* church, and by which all our clergy, in all future ages, fhould be fummarily concluded, we fhall, I fuppofe, fee juft reafon to wifh, that they had been more equal than they appear to be, to fo weighty an undertaking. Thofe who are well acquainted with their writings, will fee, in a variety of inftances, evident marks of their infufficiency for fuch a tafk, and be fully convinced of the truth of that obfervation of a learned and worthy doctor of our church, that they were but *bad interpreters of the fcriptures.*

ARCHBISHOP *Cranmer*, it is well known, had the principal hand as a divine, in conducting the great work of our reformation. In the reign of King *Edward* VI. (1548) he publifhed a *catechifm,* or *fhort inftruction into Chriftian religion,* prefixing to it a dedication to his Majefty. The following extracts from that treatife, will afford matter of fpeculation to the curious, and at the fame time of conviction to the judicious, that one of the moft learned and beft men in *England* was defective in a branch

of

of literature that moſt concerned him, and
was far ſhort of thoſe attainments in bibli-
cal knowledge, and the genuine ſenſe of
Scripture, of which the preſent age is ſo
happily poſſeſſed.—Judge from what you
read under the following heads.

I. *Original Sin.*

" IN the ninth and tenth commandments
you ſhall learn, that evil luſts and appetites which come unto us from our firſt
father *Adam* be ſins, and that no man or
woman, no not infants in their mother's
womb, do live without ſuch luſts and appetites.—Theſe appetites and deſires we
may perceive to be even in infants which
lie in their cradle. For when ſuch young
babes do not lie ſoftly, or be grieved with
thirſt, hunger or cold, they cry unpatient-
ly. Likewiſe when we ſhew them any
pleaſant thing to their eyes, and ſuddenly
again take it from them, we ſee them weep.
And theſe be plain and evident tokens, that
infants newly born be given to their own
wills and appetites, and are ſinners, for as
much as they tranſgreſs this commandment,
Thou ſhalt not deſire.—Let not the ſayings
of certain unlearned perſons move you,
which affirm that infants and ſuch as be
under the years of diſcretion, are pure, innocent

:nocent and clean without fin. For this
opinion is not true, nor agreeable to holy
Scripture : and they that fay fo, deceive both
themfelves and other. For infants are baptized for this purpofe, that they by the
fame may . enjoy remiffion of their fins.
. And in cafe they needed not forgivenefs of.
their offences, then they had no need to be
chriftened. But there be few that under-
ftandeth this doctrine. For man's reafon
cannot attain to it, neither can it comprehend how infants fhould be finners by the
reafon . of lufts and defires, called concupifcence, in the which they be conceived and
born ; but they that lean to their natural
wit, judgeth young babes to be-innocent
and void of fin, becaufe they commit no
outward offence, or actual fin. But we in
this cafe muft not judge after our *reafon*,
but according to the word of God, which
evidently declareth unto us, that concupifcence is fin.—And to know this thing,
is a point of high wifdom, to the which
every man doth not attain. For the apoftle
Paul doth confefs, that he had not known
this fin, if the law had not given him
warning of it *. For he faith, I had not

* Can we fuppofe that the worthy author underftood St.
Paul here in his true fenfe ? Or are we obliged to adopt
and adhere to the author's interpretation ?.

known

known concupifcence, if the law had not faid, Thou fhalt not defire or luft. Wherefore lock up this leffon in the coffer of your memories, by the which you fhall learn truly to fear God."

" Our firft parents *Adam* and *Eve*, [being] poifoned with the venom of the ferpent—were replenifhed with concupifcence, and evil defires, lufts and appetites. And thefe be the roots of original fin, out of the which all other fins do fpring and grow. So *Adam* and *Eve* had a very great fall, that fell from God's benediction, favour and love, into God's curfe, anger and difpleafure ; that fell from original juftice into original fin, by the which fall, all the ftrength and powers both of their bodies and fouls were fore decayed and corrupted. And as our firft parents *Adam* and *Eve* were infected and corrupted, even fo be we, that be their children. For as we fee by daily experience, that commonly gouty parents begetteth gouty children ; and if the father and the mother be infected with the leprie, we fee commonly that the children born between them have the felf-fame difeafe : So likewife, as our firft parents *Adam* and *Eve* did not put their truft in God, no more do they, that be carnally born of them. And as they loved not God, fo
their

their children love him not : And as they
followed their own concupifcence, lufts
and appetites, and not the will of God,
even fo do all their iffue. So that all
their pofterity upon earth be finners, even
in their mothers wombs.—And for this
caufe the Scripture doth fay, that all we
are conceived and born in fin. (*Pfal.* 51.)
And St. *Paul* faith (*Eph.* 2.) that by nature we be the children of God's wrath.
So that we all fhould everlaftingly be
damned, if Chrift by his death had not
redeemed us."—

" The well and head out of the which
all the evils in this miferable world do
fpring, is original fin ; in the which we
were conceived and born in our mothers
wombs, whereby man's *reafon* is fo blinded,
that of himfelf he cannot know God, nor
his word. And man's *will* alfo by this fin
is fo poifoned, that he doth not obey the
will of God, nor keep his commandments ;—nay, we feel in ourfelves, that
even from our tender age, and in our cra-
dles alfo, we be clean contrary-minded to
the will of God."

[In fhort, men in thofe times had fuch
dreadful notions of *original fin*, that, as
Bifhop *Latimer* tells us, fome thought it to
be

be the *fin againft the Holy Ghoft*. And aocord-
ingly we may think it well for us in thefe
times (and a happy efcape it was) that the
compilers of the articles did not begin their
ninth in fome fuch words as thefe : *Original, or birth-fin* (which is the fin againft
the Holy Ghoft) *ftandeth not*, &c,]

II. *Baptifm.*

" THESE be the words of our Lord
Jefus Chrift, fpoken to his difciples : *Go
into the whole world, and teache all nations,*
and baptize them, in the *name of the Father, and the Sonne, and the Holi Goft.* By
thefe words our Lord Jefus Chrift did inftitute baptifm, whereby we be·born again
to the kingdom·of God."—" By baptifm
we be born again to a new and heavenly
life, and be received into God's church
and congregation, which is the foundation
and pillar of the truth.—The caufe of this
our fecond birth, is the finfulnefs and fil-
thinefs of our firft birth. For by our firft
nativity (when we were born of our fathers
and mothers) all we were born in fin ; and
when we iffued out of our mothers womb,
we were laden with fin and God's anger.
For as *Adam* did fin, and by fin was fo
corrupted both in his body and foul, that
by his own power or ftrength he was not
F able

able to do any good thing, even fo all the
children and offspring of *Adam* be born
finners, fo that they cannot be juftified by
themfelves, or by their own ftrength, but
are inclined and bent to fin at all times;
(Eph. 2.) But when we be born again by
baptifm, then our fins be forgiven us, and
the Holy Ghoft is given us, which doth
make us alfo holy.—By baptifm we be
made the children of God, and receive the
Holy Ghoft, which doth help us to withftand all evil, and to do that is good.—"

" BAPTISM is not water alone, and nothing elfe befides, but it is the water of
God, and hath his (its) ftrength by the
word of God, and is a feal of God's promife. Wherefore it doth work in us all
thofe things, whereunto God hath ordained
it. For our Lord Jefus Chrift faith, Go and
baptize all nations, &c. This God commanded his difciples to do. Wherefore by
the virtue of this commandment, which
came from Heaven, even from the bofom
of God, baptifm doth work in us, as the
work of God. For when we be baptized
in the name of God, that is as much as to
fay, as God himfelf fhould baptize us,
Wherefore we ought not to have an eye
only to the water, but to God rather,
which did ordain the baptifm of water,
and

and commanded it to be done in his name.
For he is Almighty, and able to work in
us by baptifm, forgivenefs of our fins, and
all thofe wonderful effects and operations,
for the which he hath ordained the fame.

"Therefore confider the great treafures
and benefits, whereof God maketh us partakers, when we are baptifed, which be
thefe.

" The *firft* is, that in baptifm, our fins
be forgiven us; as St. *Peter* witnefleth,
faying; Let every one of you be baptized
for the forgivenefs of his fins. The *fecond*
is, that the Holy Ghoft is given us, the
which doth fpread abroad the love of God
in our heart, whereby we may keep God's
commandments, according to the faying of
St. *Peter (Actuum 2.)* Let every one of
you be baptifed in the name of Chrift, and
then you fhall receive the gift of the Holy
Ghoft. The *third* is, that by baptifm the
whole righteoufnefs of Chrift is given unto
us, that we may claim the fame as our
own. For fo St. *Paul* teacheth, faying; As
many of ye as are baptized in Chrift, have
put upon you Chrift. [A Chriftian man
hath the certain word of God, whereupon
he may ground his confcience that he is
made a Chriftian man, and is one of Chrift's

mem-

members, which he is assured of by baptism. For he that is baptized, may assuredly say thus : " I am not now in this waver-
" ing opinion, that I only suppose myself
" to be a Christian man, but I am in a
" sure belief, that I am made a Christian
" man. For I know for a surety that I am
" baptized; and I am sure also, that bap-
" tism was ordained of God, and that he
" which baptized me, did it by God's
" commission and commandment. And
" the Holy Ghost doth witness, that he
" which is baptized, hath put upon him
" Christ. Wherefore the Holy Ghost in
" my baptism assureth me, that I am a
" Christian man." And this is a true and
sincere faith, which is able to stand against
the gates of hell, for as much as it hath
for it the evidence of God's word, and
leaneth not to any man's saying or opinion.]
—*Fourthly*, by baptism we die with Christ,
and are buried (as it were) in his blood and
death, that we should suffer afflictions and
death as Christ himself hath suffered. And
as that man which is baptized, doth promise
to God that he will die with Christ, that
he may be dead to sin, and to the old
Adam; so on the other part, God doth
promise again to him, that he shall be partaker of Christ's death and passion. [—God
doth forgive us our sins by faith, but by
afflic-

afflictions and death he doth take them clean away, as St. *Peter* witnesseth, saying; He that suffereth, or is afflicted in the flesh, doth cease from sin. And St. *Paul* sayeth, He that is dead is justified, or delivered from sin. These be the promises which we make when we are baptized.]

" By this which I have spoken, I trust you understand, wherefore baptism is called the bath of regeneration, and how in baptism we be born again, and be made new creatures.—Before we were baptized, it is evident that we were sinners; and he that is a sinner, can have no peace nor quietness of conscience before he come to Christ; so much he feareth God's wrath and everlasting damnation. But after that our sins, in baptism be forgiven us, and we believe the promise of God, and so by our faith be justified, then our consciences be quieted, and we be glad and merry, trusting assuredly, that God is no more angry with us for our former offences, and that we shall not be damned for the same. And this is a marvellous alteration, and renewing of the inward man; the which could be wrought by the power of no creature, but by God alone.

" Also before we were baptized, we were

F 3   slaves

flaves and bondmen to fin, fo that we neither could do that good which we would have done, nor could keep us from that evil which we would not have done, as St. *Paul* complaineth of himfelf, *Rom.* 7. *
But when by baptifm the Holy Ghoft was given us, the which did fpread abroad the love of God in our hearts, and did alfo deliver us from the bondage and tyranny of fin, and gave us new ftrength and power to wreftle againft fin, and manfully to withftand our ghoftly enemy the Devil, then, after a certain manner, we were able to fulfil God's commandments. And this is a great change and renewing of the inward man.—Know for a furety, and ftedfaftly believe, that no child of the *Jews* or *Turks,* which is not baptized, hath the Holy Ghoft, neither that any fuch can underftand the word of God, neither that any fuch is holy or righteous before God."

III. *Imputed Righteoufnefs.*

" HE that is a finner and not baptized,

---

* Here is a ftrong inftance, amongft many others, of the injudicious and inconfiftent manner of interpreting the Scripture in thofe times. The learned of the prefent age, with much better reafon, underftand the matter otherwife. See Dr. *Whitby*'s note on the 25th verfe of this chapter.

although

although he had the Holy Ghost to this
effect, *(viz)* to help him to fight against
fin, yet oftentimes he is overcome, and
falleth to fin,—and he is ever in peril left
he be overcome of fin :—but when in baptifm the righteoufnefs of Chrift is given
and-imputed to him, then he is delivered
from all thofe perils. For he knoweth
for a furety, that he hath put upon him
Chrift, and that his weaknefs and imperfection is covered and hid with the perfect righteoufnefs and holinefs of Chrift.
Wherefore after baptifm he doth not truft
in his own righteoufnefs, but in Chrift only.
And he is no more penfive or doubtful,
confidering his own weaknefs, but he is
joyful, becaufe he confidereth that he is
made partaker of Chrift's righteoufnefs.—
Seeing that Chrift was the moft innocent
lamb, that never was blotted with any fpot
of fin, and yet he fuffered for us as a finner, it is evident hereby, that he died not
for himfelf, but took upon him our fins,
and bore for us the burden which we fhould
have borne.—Hereby we may evidently
perceive, that the great wrath and indignation of God to us hath an end, and that
by our lively faith in Chrift, our fins be
forgiven us, and that we be reconciled into
the favour of God, made holy and righteous. For then God doth no more impute

unto

unto us our former fins, but he doth impute and give unto us the juftice and
righteoufnefs of his fon Jefus Chrift, which
fuffered for us.—

" God caufeth his gofpel to be preached unto us,—he openeth our hearts, and
giveth us faith to believe his gofpel. And
to them that believe his gofpel he giveth
the Holy Ghoft, which doth govern us,
and lead us unto all truth.—By faith we
be juftified before God; for faith maketh
us partakers of the juftice of Chrift, and
planteth us in Chrift; and he that by true
faith do receive the promife of grace, to
him God giveth the Holy Ghoft; by whom
charity is fpread abroad in our hearts,
which performeth all the commandments.
Therefore he that believeth in Chrift, and
truly believeth the gofpel, he is juft and
holy before God, by the juftice of Chrift,
which is imputed and given unto him, as
St. *Paul* faith, *Rom.* 3."

It may be noted here, that imputed
righteoufnefs is fet by this author in oppofition to the ftrict demands of the *law*, but
not in St. *Paul*'s fenfe of either, which, fince
this worthy man's time, has been made
abundantly evident by perfons of the greateft
accuracy and difcernment. The archbifhop
seems

feems to have underftood the apoftle as fpeaking only of the *moral law*, particularly, as he exprefsly afferts, of the ten commandments, which, faith he, " are an excellent godly, and heavenly doctrine, but by them we do only learn what God requireth of us, and fo be brought to the knowledge of our fin. For this is the office of the *law*, to teach us our offences, and to fet before our eyes the great fear of God, and the indignation which we have deferved by breaking his commandments;" —with other pofitions of this kind, and inferences properly drawn from them; all honeftly meant, but in refpect of the argument, and the term *law*, not exhibiting the *true* fenfe and defign of fcripture.

As to the tenet of *imputed righteoufnefs*, it made a great noife in the world in former times, and is now again infifted upon anew by fome zealous revivers of the Calvinian doctrines, who exactly tread in the fteps of the famous Dr. *Owen* and his followers. But the peculiar notions on this head, owing to a wrong interpretation of fcripture, were thoroughly refuted long ago, in a valuable treatife, intitled, *A difcourfe concerning the imputation of Chrift's righteoufnefs to us, and our fins to him, &c.* Written by Mr. *Hotchkis*, a learned clergyman in *Wilts*: which

all

all the fyftematical artifices in the world will never be able to overthrow.

IV. *As to the Three Sacraments.*

" Our lord Jefus Chrift hath inftituted and annexed to the gofpel, *three* facraments, or holy feals of his covenant and league made with us. And by thefe three, God's minifters do work with us in the name and place of God (yea God himfelf worketh with us) to confirm us in our faith, and to afferten us that we are the lively members of God's true church, and the chofen people of God to whom the gofpel is fent; and that all thofe things belong to us, whereof the promifes of the gofpel make mention. " The firft of thefe facraments is *baptifm*;" which hath been already treated upon. " The fecond is *abfolution*;" of which under the next head. " And the third is the *communion*," or the Lord's-fupper; of which in due place hereafter.

V. *Abfolution.*

" By abfolution, or the authority of the keys, we be abfolved from fuch fins as we be fallen into after our baptifm. — When we fall again to great fins after that we are once baptized, we ought not to negleét it,

nor

nor by walking in a certain rechelefnes,
think that our fins be forgiven us only becaufe God is merciful; but in the fight
between our confcience (on the one hand)
and the devil (on the other, fuggefting fuch
a notion,) our great truft and comfort is,
the fure word and work of God, which
may afcertain us that our fins are forgiven,
that is to fay, when we obtain forgivenefs
of our fins by fure truft in God's mercy,
and as time ferveth to feek for abfolution of
the minifters of the church, to whom Chrift
hath delivered the keys.——Now when a
man, after baptifm, hath grievoufly finned,
and doubteth in his confcience whether he
be in the favour of God or no (as oftentimes
it happeneth) then it is hard for him to
truft to his own imaginations, thinking on
this fafhion, ' I know I have finned, but
' yet I am in this opinion, that God is not fo
' cruel a revenger, but that he hath for-
' given.' For fuch an opinion, without God's
word, is not a true faith, nor is able to
ftand in the dangerous fkirmifhes of temptation : but true faith muft ever be ftayed
upon the certain word and work of God.
Now God doth not fpeak to us with a voice
founding out of heaven ; but he hath given
the keys of the kingdom of heaven, and the
authority to forgive fin, to the minifters of
the church. Wherefore let him that is a
finner

finner go to one of them, let him knowledge and confefs his fin, and pray him that
according to God's commandment, he will
give him abfolution, and comfort him with
the word of grace, and forgivenefs of his
fins.

. " AND when the minifter doth fo, then
I ought ftedfaftly to believe, that my fins
are truely forgiven me in heaven. And fuch
a faith is able to ftand ftrong in all fkirmifhes and affaults of our mortal enemy the
devil, forafmuch as it is builded upon a
rock, that is to fay, upon the certen word
of God. For he that is abfolved, knoweth
for a furety, that his fins be forgiven him
by the minifter. And he knoweth affuredly
alfo, that the minifter hath authority from
God himfelf fo to do. And thirdly, he
knoweth that God hath made this promife
to his minifters, and faid to them, To whom
ye forgive fins upon earth, to him alfo they
fhall be forgiven in heaven. Wherefore
give good ear to this doctrine, and when
your fins do make you afraid and fad, then
feek and defire abfolution and forgivenefs
of your fins, of the minifters, which have
received a commiffion and commandment
from Chrift himfelf to forgive men their
fins, and then your confciences fhall have
peace, tranquillity and quietnefs. But he
that doth not obey this counfel, but being
either

either blind or proud, doth defpife the
fame, he fhall not find forgivenefs of his
fins, neither in his own good works, nor
yet in painful chaftifements of his body, or
any other thing whereto God hath not
promifed remiffion of fins. Wherefore defpife not abfolution, for it is the commandment and ordinance of God, and the Holy
Spirit of God is prefent, and caufeth thefe
things to take effect in us, and to work our
falvation: —— infomuch that whatfoever
God's minifters do to us by God's commandment, are as much available, as if
God himfelf fhould do the fame. For
whether the minifters do excommunicate
open malefactors, and unrepentant perfons,
or do give abfolution to thofe which be
truly repentant for their fins, and amend
their lives, thefe acts of the minifters have
as great power and authority, and be confirmed and ratified in heaven, as though our
lord Jefus Chrift himfelf had done the fame.
Wherefore,—when you be afked, how underftand you the words before rehearfed,
[*whofe fins ye fhall forgive in earth, &c.*]
ye fhall anfwer, " I do believe, that whatfo-
" ever the minifters of Chrift do to us by
" God's commandment, either in excom-
" municating open and unrepentant fin-
" ners, or in abfolving repentant perfons,
" all their acts be of as great authority,
" and as furely confirmed in heaven, as if
" Chrift

" Chrift fhould fpeak the words out of
" heaven." "

" So you have the beginning and foundation of the minifters of God's word, and
of the authority of the keys, as our lord
Jefus Chrift did firft ordain and inftitute
the fame. The which our faviour Chrift
did inftitute and appoint for this purpofe,
that our confciences might thereby be com-
forted, and affured of the forgivenefs of
fins, and to have the ineftimable treafures
of the gofpel, as often as we have need
thereof; that we thereby being made ftrong
in our faith, might fo continue to the end
of our life."

VI. *Impofition of hands; Ordination;
Minifterial authority,* &c.

" THE words of Chrift be thefe *(John*
20 :) Our lord Jefus breathed on his apoftles, and faid, Receive ye the Holy Ghoft :
whofe fins ye forgive, they are forgiven unto
them, and whofe fins you referve, they are
referved.——Our faviour Chrift did breathe
into his difciples, and gave them the Holy
Ghoft. Where the Holy Ghoft is, there he
fo worketh, that he caufeth us to do thofe
things which Chrift hath commanded : and
when that is not done, then the Holy Ghoft

4   is

is not there.——After Chrift's afcenfion,
the apoftles gave authority to other godly
and holy men, to minifter God's word. —
Where they found godly men, and meet to
preach God's word, they laid their hands
upon them, and gave them the Holy Ghoft,
as they themfelves received of Chrift the
fame Holy Ghoft, to execute this office. And
they that were fo ordained, were indeed,
and alfo were called, the minifters of God,
as the apoftles themfelves were. And fo
the miniftration of God's word (which our
lord Jefus Chrift himfelf did firft inftitute)
was derived from the apoftles unto other after them, by impofition of hands, and giving the Holy Ghoft, from the apoftles time
to our days. And this was the confecration, orders and unction of the apoftles,
whereby they, at the beginning, made bifhops and priefts, and this fhall continue in
the church even to the world's end *.

" Wherefore you fhall give due re-
verence and honour to the minifters of the
church, and fhall not meanly or lightly
efteem them in the execution of their office,

---

* Then follows this remark; " And whatfoever rite or
ceremony hath been added more than this, cometh of man's
ordinance and policy, and is not commanded by God's
word."

but

but you fhall take them for God's miniftefs, and the meffengers of our lord Jefus Chrift. For Chrift himfelf faith in the gofpel, He that heareth You, heareth Me, and he that defpifeth You, defpifeth Me. Wherefore you fhall ftedfaftly believe all thofe things which minifters fhall fpeak unto you from the mouth, and by the commandment of our lord Jefus Chrift. And whatfoever they do to you, as when they baptize you, when they give you abfolution, and diftribute to you the body and blood of our lord Jefus Chrift, thefe you fhall fo efteem as if Chrift himfelf, in his own perfon, did fpeak and minifter unto you.——All things which the minifters of the church do fay or do to us, ought to be directed to this end, that they may loofe us, and declare unto us the forgivenefs of our fins, when we truly repent, and believe in Chrift. But when we do not repent us of our fin, and forfake the fame, or do not believe the gofpel, then they ought to bind or referve fin, and to declare unto us, that if we ftill continue in fin, we fhall be damned for ever. And when the minifters do thus execute their commiffion, then they obey God, and whofe fins foever they forgive in earth, their fins be forgiven in heaven alfo. And contrari-wife, whomfoever they bind in earth, their fins be bound alfo in heaven;". [as was declared

clared under the article of *abfolution.*] " But
if the minifters would enterprife to do contrary to their commiffion, that is to fay, to
forgive fins to unrepentant finners and unbelievers, or to bind their fins and deny
them abfolution that be repentant, and truft
in the mercy of God, then they fhould not
do well, nor their act fhould be of any
force [18].

" But when the minifters do truly execute
their office, you ought to take great comfort, and to confirm your faith thereby,
that you may ftedfaftly believe, and in all
temptations anfwer your adverfary the devil
after this manner;

" God hath fent to me one of his mi-
" nifters : He, in the name and place of
" God, hath declared to me the forgive-
" nefs of my fins, and hath baptized me in
" the affurance of the fame. Wherefore I
" doubt not but that my fins be forgiven,
" and that I am made the fon and heir of
" God."

VII. *Satisfaction of Chrift.*

" It was requifite that Chrift, God and
man, fhould be conceived by the Holy Ghoft,
and born of a pure virgin. For if Chrift

G   fhould

should redeem us, and satisfy for our sins, then must he needs be holy and without sin. For if he had been guilty and a sinner, then could he not have holpen his own self, but he must needs have had another saviour and redeemer for him, as well as we have for us. For whatsoever he had done or suffered, should have been worthily for his own offences, and yet could he not have satisfied for other. Wherefore it was necessary, if he should satisfy for us, that his nativity should be pure without sin, and not corrupt as our's is. That our corrupt and damnable nativity might be purified and made holy, by the holy and pure nativity of Christ; therefore Christ, being pure and clean from all sin, was able to redeem sinners and satisfy for them. Now forasmuch as the justice of God did require that Christ should suffer and make satisfaction for us, and do all things that we were bound to do, it was necessary that he should be made man. For if he had not been a very natural man, he could not have done for us all those things which we were bound to do. And again, if he had not been very God, he could not have been pure and clean from all sin, and so have made a true and perfect satisfaction * for our sins. For no man can

perfectly

---

* Note: The word *satisfaction* never occurs in the new Testament; nor is the scholastic or systematic sense, in
which

perfectly fulfil the will of God, but God himself alone.—Again, if he had not been very God, he could not have loosed the bands of death, neither have raised himself from death to life.

FURTHER : "We must believe and confess this thing, that all we are conceived and born in sin. We are therefore by nature the children of God's wrath, and should be damned for ever if Christ had not redeemed us by his holy passion. For he was made man for us, and did all things for us, which we were bound to do, and could not do; that is to say, he fulfilled the *law* for us, and took upon him all that cross which we most righteously had deserved for our iniquities and offences, and he shed his blood for us, that our sins might be forgiven us. All these things we ought stedfastly to believe. Wherefore they be in a great error, which will make satisfaction for their sins with fasting, prayer, alms-deed, and such like good works. For although we are bound to do these good works, yet they be not a sufficient price, ransom or satisfaction for our sins, but onely the death and blood of our

which divines have commonly applied it, to be found there.

G 2   saviour

faviour Chrift was a fufficient and worthy
facrifice to take away our fins, and to ob-
teyne for us forgivenefs of our offences, as
it is written in the fecond chapter of St.
John his firft epiftle; Chrift is that facrifice
that pacifieth God's difpleafure, and ob-
teyneth pardon for our fins, and not for our
fins onely, but alfo for the fins of all the
world."

VIII. *Body and blood of Chrift.*

" The *third* facrament is the Communion, or the Lord's Supper, by the which
we be fed and nourifhed, and fortified in
the faith of the gofpel and knowledge of
Chrift; that by this food we may grow
more and more in newnefs of life, fo that
we may be no longer children, but may wax
perfect men, and full grown in Chrift.—

" Although Chrift prefcribeth no certen
time, when we ought to come together to
his fupper, although alfo he appoint no
certeyn number of days, how often in the
year we ought to receive this fupper, yet
this is his holy and godly will, that at *fome
time* we fhould receive this facrament.—

" We ought to believe that in the facrament, we receive truly the body and blood
of

of Chrift. · For God is almighty : he is able therefore to do all things what he will; and as St. *Paul* writeth, He calleth thofe things which be not, as if they were. Wherefore when Chrift taketh bread, and faith, 'Take, ' eat, this is my body,' we ought not to doubt but we eat his very body. And when he taketh the cup, and faith, 'Take, drink, ' this is my blood,' we ought to think af-furedly, that we drink his very blood. And this we muft believe, if we will be counted Chriften men.

" And whereas in this perilous time, certain deceitful perfons be found in many places, who of very frowardnes will not grant that it is the very body and blood of Chrift, but deny the fame, for none other caufe, but that they cannot compafs by man's blind reafon, how this thing fhould be brought to pafs, 'ye fhall with all diligence beware of fuch perfons, that ye fuffer not yourfelves to be deceived by them. For fuch men furely are not true Chriftians, neither as yet have they learned the firft article of the creed, which teacheth that God is almighty. Wherefore efchew fuch erroneous opinions, and believe the words of our lord Jefus, that you eat and drink his very body and blood, although man's reafon cannot comprehend how and after what manner the fame is

prefent.

prefent. For the wifdom of reafon muft
be fubdu d to the obedience of Chrift, as
the apoftle *Paul* teacheth *.——

" WHEREFORE doubt not but in the
Lord's fupper we receive the body and
blood of Chrift. For he hath faid fo, and
by the power of his word hath caufed it
fo to be. Wherefore feeing Chrift faith,
' Do this, as often as ye do it, in remem-
' brance of me,' it is evident hereby, that
Chrift caufeth, even at this time, his body
and blood to be in the facrament after that
manner and fafhion as it was at that time,
when he made his Maundye [or celebrated
his laft fupper] with his difciples. For elfe
we could not do that thing which his difciples did. But Chrift hath commanded us
to do the felf-fame thing that his difciples
did, and to do it in the remembrance of
him, that is to fay, to receive his body and
blood, even fo as he himfelf did give it to
his difciples. And let not the foolifh talk
of unbelievers move you, who are wont to
afk this queftion; ' How can the prieft or
minifter make the body and blood of Chrift?'

* To what part of *Paul's* teachings can we fuppofe the
bifhop here to allude?——If to 1 *Cor.* i. let us judge as
favourably as we can of the mifapprehenfion of fo great
and good a man.

To

To which I anſwer, that the miniſter doth not this, but Chriſt himſelf doth give unto us his fleſh and blood, as his words doth evidently declare. — 'When ye ſhall have examined yourſelves, ye ſhall find that ye are ſinners, and that ye have need that Chriſt ſhould give his body for you, and ſhed his blood for you. And this to do, is truly to examine and try yourſelves: —when ye do thus, then ye worthily receive the body and blood of Chriſt; and he that ſo receiveth it, receiveth everlaſting life. For he doth not with his bodily mouth receive the body and blood of Chriſt, but he doth believe the words of Chriſt, whereby he is aſſured, that Chriſt's body was given to death for us, and that his blood was ſhed for us. - And he that thus believeth, eateth and drinketh the body and blood of Chriſt *ſpiritually*.' [This, by the way, ſeems to be a ſtrange turn given all on the ſudden to thoſe ſtrong words ſo much before inſiſted on, viz. ' *the very body, the very blood;— doing the ſelf-ſame thing which the diſciples did;*' that is to ſay, receiving his body and blood even ſo as He himſelf did give it to them, &c. Now all this corporiety is ſpiritualized, and it is not very eaſy to make the two accounts conſiſtent.——To confirm this latter opinion, according to his interpretation of ſcripture (plainly miſapplying it here, as is now well known to the learn-

ed,)

ed,) this good man subjoins as follows,
" Of this *spiritual* eating, &c. Christ speak-
eth when he saith (*John.* vi. *). ' He that
eateth my flesh, and drinketh my blood,
abideth in me, and I in him.' And when
we be planted in Christ, then we may come
to this holy supper as often as we will, that
by this *ghostly* food we may daily more and
more wax stronger in our faith, that Christ
was given to be the ransom for our sins,
and that he dwelleth in us, and we in
him.———

" SEEING our saviour Christ doth give
us his body to be our meat, and his blood
to be our drink, and thereby doth declare

---

* The reformers all to a man understood this sixth chapter of St. *John* as treating of the *Lord's supper*, (though
that, by the way, is no reason why we should understand
it so too :) Thus in their *necessary erudition of a Christian
man* 1543, (which Mr. *Strype* says was chiefly of the archbishop's composing,) they have these words in their comment on the 4th petition of the Lord's prayer:

" By this bread, which we be taught to aske in thus Petition, may be understande the holy sacramente of the aultare,
the very flesshe and bloude of our saviour Jesu Christ, as it is
written in the vi chapiter of Sainte John ; " I am the breade of
lyfe, whiche came down from heaven. And the breade whiche
I wyll gyue, is my flesshe, whiche I wyll gyue for the lyfe of
the worlde." And in this prayer we desyre, that the same
maye be purely minystered, and distributed to the comfort and
benefite of al vs, the true children of God."

4   that

that he will effectually dwell in us, strengthen
and preferve us to everlafting life, we may
ftedfaftly believe that Chrift doth work in
us, and that he will give us ghoftly ftrength
and ftedfaftnefs, &c. And this is the meaning and plain underftanding of the words
of the Lord's fupper.—Wherefore when
ye be afked, What is the communion or
the Lord's fupper, ye may anfwer, " It is
the true body, and true blood of our Lord
Jefus Chrift, which was ordained by Chrift
himfelf to be eaten and drunken of us
Chriftian people under bread and wine.—
So ye have the true underftanding of the
words of Chrift, and the true ufe of the
holy fupper of the Lord."

See the *Communion-Office.*

IX. *Chrift's defcent into hell.*

THE original word *hades* is now fufficiently underftood by the learned, which at
the time of the reformation, and long after, it was not. Archbifhop *Cranmer* underftood κατελθοντα 'εις αδυ, of the *local*
defcent of Chrift into the place of tor-
ment; and fo did the famous Dr. *Peter*
Heylin, who with fufficient affurance attacked the incomparably learned archbifhop
Ufher on this head, who underftood the
matter better than both, and is now fe-
conded

conded by all the best critics in *Europe*.
—Our good reformer's words are these :
" Our Lord Jesus Christ was very God,
and very man. As man he suffered death
for us, and descended into *hell*. But as naturally God, he loosed the bonds and pains
of hell, he destroyed the kingdom of death,
he rose from death to life, and so paid the
ransom for our sins, and taketh away all
the guiltiness of the same."

This doctrine, it must be owned, continued in the church a long time after, tho'
rather heightened in some particulars. It
may be worth while to see how the learned
Dr. *Fulke* expresses the common belief concerning this article in his time. " *We do
constantly believe the article of our Creed that
our Saviour Christ descended into* hell, *by
suffering in soul the paynes due to* God's juftice, *for the sins of all whom he redeemed,
and by vanquishing the* Devil, *and all the
power of hell, in working the redemption of
all the children of* God." Defence of the
English translations of the bible against
Martin, 1583, ch. 7, where he takes notice of " maister *Latimer*'s error, as he calls
it, of Christ's suffering *torments* in hell,
&c."

See a curious note of Dr. *Nichols* on this
subject, under the epistle for Easter-even.

X.

X. *Power of the Devil.*

" BECAUSE man's reason is blinded, it is easy for the Devil to lead man to all errors, as idolatry, heresies, witchcrafts, enchantments, and to all kind of superstitious and false doctrine. And these offences God doth punish with diverse and grievous plagues ; as with pride, envy, contencyon, detraction, slandering, lying, railing, &c. And hereof ensue divers diseases, sicknesses, &c. Also when man's will is not ruled by God's law, he runneth headlong into all kind of gross and horrible sin, as treason, sedition, adulteries, theft, extortion, &c. And because God of his justice cannot suffer such heinous sins unpunished, therefore he suffereth the Devil sometime to infect the air, sometime to stir up great and dangerous tempests and storms, sometime he permitteth him to destroy our houses, cattle, and riches, with fire or water. Again, God suffereth him sometime to have such power over us for our sins, that some he maketh to run mad, some he causeth to drown themselves, some to burn themselves, some to cut their own throats, some hang themselves. For this is Satan's chief study, to drive men to such fear, trouble, and anguish of mind, that through pensiveness,

and

and heavinefs of heart, he may bring them
to defperation. And this is his only intent
and ftudy, to bring as many as he can to
everlafting damnation.

Thus " you have heard into how great
and horrible evils we be brought unto by
Original Sin, fo that everi moment we be
in danger to be drowned with the ragious
floods thereof."

IF to the foregoing extracts, taken from
the archbifhop's *catechifm*, we fubjoin his
unhappy notion concerning the enormous
fupremacy of the regal power, in religious
as well as civil affairs, we fhall be inclined
to think (with all due refpect to his real
merits) that his grace was not more infallible in this, than he was in fome of thofe
other articles, which have been above produced. The account we have of the matter, in fhort, is this. Some of our reformers, in their zeal againft the papal fupremacy, ftretched the regal to fuch an ex-
orbitant height, as to reduce the church to
be a mere creature of the ftate ; and to declare that the King is the fountain of all
authority, civil and ecclefiaftical ; and that
it is lawful for him to revoke fuch authority at pleafure. At the head of thofe who
entertained and avowed this opinion, was
the

the good archbifhop *Cranmer*. But Mr.
Strype and others affure us, that on farther
confideration, and conference with bifhop
Ridley, he relinquifhed that error.—This
then being the cafe, what fhall we fay to
Dr. *Balguy*, who feems fond of reviving
that error, and giving it a frefh polifh, in
an age when it was thought to have been
covered over with ruft, and never like to
have been fcoured up again, and recommended to the world for true fterling divinity of the church of *England?*

REFLECTIONS

ON THE FOREGOING EXTRACTS.

1. ONE very obvious reflection occurring
on a furvey of the whole is this;
that the proteftant religion being then in
its infancy, and not fufficiently purged from
erroneous doctrines, which our reformers
had imbibed in their earlier, and were too
fond of retaining in their riper years, it
was rather too hafty a ftep taken by them,
to draw up a fyftem of doctrines which
fhould tie down the belief of their fellow-
proteftants to the precife meafure and dimenfion

menfion of their own, and efpecially fo as to include pofterity alfo in the ftrait inclofure. An attempt of this kind, for which they had no authority from God, tho' they had from the ftate, would have been better poftponed to more enlightened times, if to any.

2. THERE was one thing fomewhat incongruous in the conduct of thefe reformers, that whilft they profeffed to make the holy *fcriptures* the rule of their reformation, they too often varied from the true meaning and defign of thofe fcriptures, and yet openly declared, that in their expofitions, they had given the world the true fenfe of them. Thus in the dedication of their *Inftitution of a Chriften man* to King *Henry* VIII. (1537,) they affure his Majefty, that " having determined their " fentence in all things contained in their " treatife, according to the very true mean- " ing of fcripture, we do offer (fay they) " the fame herewith unto your moft ex- " cellent Majefty, moft humbly befeech- " ing the fame to permit and fuffer it, in " cafe it fhall be fo thought meet to your " moft excellent wifdom, to be printed, " and fo with your fupreme power fet " forth." But is it not feemingly a ftrange piece of inconfiftence, after averring that they had given the *very true meaning of fcrip-*

scripture, they should yet, immediately after, submit that very true meaning to be altered and corrected by the King ? ". And " albeit, most dread and benigne soveraign " Lorde, we do affirm by our lernynges " with one consent, that the said treatise " is in all points so concordant and agree- " able to holy scripture, as we trust your " Majesty shall receive the same, as a thing " most sincerely and purely handled to the " glory of God, your grace's honour, tho " unity of your people, the which things " your highnefs we may well fee and per- " ceive, doth chiefly in the fame desire : " yet we do most humbly submit it to tho " most excellent wisdom and exact juge- " ment of your Majesty, to be recognifed, " overseen, and corrected," &c. And yet, to give proof of their imperfection in divi- nity, and conviction of some mistakes they had made in the foregoing treatise, did they not, a few years after, acknowlege their mistakes, by rectifying several things there- in, which, upon farther inquiry, they plain- ly discerned to be erroneous ? as appears by comparing the *Necessary Erudition,* which came out about five years after, with the preceding *Institution.* And did not *Cran- mer* himself fee reafon to change his former opinion concerning the elements in the Lord's fupper, when he came to examine

the

the matter more accurately, perceiving the
untenableness of what he had maintained
before on that head?—Thefe are fufficient
evidences of the impuberty of their underftandings in divine things, when they took
upon them to prefcribe to the underftandings of others, and, that their affuming
that office was premature.

3. It was not to be expected that men,
who had fo long fat in darknefs and in the
fhadow of death, fhould be able all at
once to tranfplant themfelves into the regi-
ons of light and truth. They opened their
eyes but gradually to difcern that light, and,
if they had lived in thefe times, it cannot
be doubted but they would have underftood
the fcriptures better, and rejected feveral
human crudities, which they then fuppofed to be divine verities.—And as to
Cranmer in particular, every one acquainted
with his hiftory, knows that he was a fincere lover of truth, one that diligently
fought it, and gladly embraced it when he
found it, though he fometimes miffed of
it, after all his fearches. Had his lot fallen
in thefe times, he would without queftion
have had different fentiments from what he
had, in many points relating to religion;
and would either not have projected any articles at all concerning it, or would have
made

made thofe he compiled, much fewer than
they are, and more conformable to fcripture, confidered in its true fenfe and latitude. Nor can we well fuppofe, that being fo honeft and unprejudiced a man as he
was, and fo thoroughly devoted to the interefts of truth, wherever he could difcern
it, it would have been in his power to have
withftood the force of the arguments which
have been fo ftrongly urged of late years in
favour of religious liberty, and in oppofition
to the enjoining of confeffions, and of fubfcriptions to them.

4. WITH regard to the *catechifm* fo
often mentioned, fuppofe the good archbifhop had judged it advifeable (with the
confent of the civil powers) to require *fubfcription* to that catechifm, as he did to the
articles, and other ecclefiaftical determinations ; or fuppofe fuch a propofal now made:
would not many judicious and confcientious
men fcruple fuch a fubfcription? would
not many remonftrate againft the propofal,
and urge cogent reafons for fuppreffing it?
—There are indeed many excellent things
in that catechifm, which muft pleafe every
man of true piety and integrity. A native
plainnefs, fimplicity and honefty, the cha-
racteriftics of all his writings, appear in
the whole performance; and it is a good

H   pattern

pattern for the clergy to follow in their catechetical inftructions to the young and ignorant. There are at the fame time, it muft be confeffed, in this compofition, fome things made up of fuch coarfe materials (as you have in part feen above) that I can by no means recommend them: And if that catechifm, or thofe doctrines, were now re-introduced, and taught anew in our churches, what would be the confequence? Would our congregations relifh them? Would they not rather be furprifed, and ftare, exclaim againft them as ftrange and unheard of doctrines, run out of our churches, and forbear frequenting them any longer?

5. And yet I am perfuaded that there are a fet of men at this time in thefe kingdoms, who would approve of all thofe extracts, readily fubfcribe them, and ardently preach them. Nor probably would there be wanting, even among thofe who affect to be reputed our moft orthodox and ftanch churchmen, fome who would as readily do the fame, and ftrenuoufly abet and defend every article, both from the prefs, and from the pulpit. Such are the various humours and turns of mens minds, efpecially when they take any odd conceit into their heads, about what they efteem religion:

They

They feed upon opinions, errors, dreams,
And make or think *them truths.*

6. SUPPOSE, upon this occasion, it be
queried, what deference the archbishop
might judge to be due to the doctrines delivered in his catechism, or to any other
such human instructions in matters of religion? the answer must be, that his own
rule, expressed in his own words, in this
very catechism, resolves the query sufficiently: in which, as well as in the sixth
article, he expresly and plainly teaches,
that all human doctrines and expositions in
such matters, must refer ultimately to, and
be decided by, the word of God; this
alone being the final test of all points delivered as Christian doctrines.

THESE are his declarations in different
places.

" TRUE faith must ever be staid upon
the certain word and work of God."

" A CHRISTIAN man ought to believe
nothing as an article of his faith, except he
be assured, that either it is God's commandment or his word."

" OUR Lord Jesus Christ hath given his
H 2   ministers

minifters plain inftructions, what they ought
to teach and do. And if they teach or do
any other thing than is contained in their
commiffion, then it is of no force, nor
ought we to regard it."—Thefe propofiti-
ons are undeniable. Many honeft and
learned proteftants do juftly wifh, that all
our articles were equally fo.

7. Upon the whole, it is fufficiently
evident, on a careful furvey of the foregoing extracts and obfervations, that it was
an ill-timed refolution taken by our reformers, to draw up articles to be the ftandards
of doctrine, at a time when they were not
duly qualified for fuch a work ; at a crifis
when they faw many things in the theology
of the times, but as through a glafs darkly ;
and confequently when they could not rea-
fonably demand fubfcription to what was
not clear and evident, and which they
could be fure the facred fcripture would
thoroughly warrant, being taken in its native fenfe : which fenfe it was the duty of
Chriftians to inquire after to the utmoft,
and to adhere to with fteadinefs when dif-
covered, after having made an honeft and
faithful fearch to this purpofe.

Would our reformers themfelves have
liked to be fo treated by others ? How did
they

they relifh the act of fix articles (only fix) when impofed upon them by the ruling powers? whom they could not refift; and if they yielded, they could not do it, we may fuppofe, without fome reluctance, perhaps a great one. And therefore *Latimer* and *Shaxton*, finding their confciences would not permit them to comply, very honeftly quitted their refpective bifhopricks.

SUBSCRIPTIONS have ftuck with many from that time to this. We hardly ever heard of fubfcription by *proxy*, either propofed or permitted to be made by the clergy, in thefe later ages of the church. And yet we are well affured, that in former times, emperors, kings, and generally all Chriftians, fubfcribed to the decrees of the church, either by themfelves, or by their fubftitutes. I fay nothing about the propriety of fuch a fubfcription, nor do I think it would be to the honour or intereft of religion to permit it to take place and be practifed in the church. Much more honourable and more juftifiable methods may be thought of to give eafe to tender confciences. And after all, the beft remedy perhaps would be, the total abolifhment of all fubfcriptions. That well known obfervation of bifhop *Burnet* will always hold

H 3   true,

true, *viz. Churches and societies are much better secured by laws, than by subscriptions.*

As to the proper time for difmiffing thefe encroachments upon Chriftian liberty, that act of honourable indulgence to their fubjects (however earneftly to be wifhed for) muft be fubmitted to the wifdom of our governors.

To every thing there is a feafon, and a time to every purpofe under heaven [1].

N[2]

N° V.

Thoughts on subscriptions required from the clergy.

IT is allowed on all hands that the *Apostles Creed* is a complete summary of Christian faith and doctrine *. The basis upon which that Creed is erected, and from which its articles are deduced, is the holy *scripture.*—Is the scripture to be interpreted by this creed, or this creed by the scripture ? Judge which of the two is the most probable and the most reasonable ; the one being of divine authority, the other of no higher origin than human.

THE declarations on this head, made by those two great men, Bishop *Pearson*, and the late Lord *King*, deserve regard.

THE former, having well considered the matter, declares it as his judgement, " That whatsoever is delivered in the *creed*, we must therefore believe, because it is contained in the *scriptures*, and consequently must *so* believe,

lieve,

lieve, as it is contained *there* :" adding, "That where the church affigns no proof from *fcripture*, fhe leaves us to *private judgement*." Exp. of the 5th. art.

THE latter, having confidered this point with equal accuracy, afferts, That every man's *private judgement* of the fenfe and meaning of the *creed*, is to be tried and determined by the holy *fcriptures*, the only perfect and infallible rule of faith; by which even the *creed* itfelf, and every explication thereof, muft be tried and judged; and they [the creed and explication,] are no farther to be received, than as they are confonant and agreeable thereto : Which is according to the fixth article of the church of *England*." *Pref. to crit. hift. of the creed*.

Now what can be faid in refutation of thefe pofitions? Can any confiftent proteftant, any fenfible and confiderate member of the church of *England* deny them? If he does, or can, he recedes from the fundamental principles of this church, and gives too much countenance to thofe of the mother of abominations, from whofe vaffalage our worthy reformers fo glorioufly recovered their Chriftian liberty, and fo carefully tranfmitted it down to Us, to preferve and maintain to the lateft pofterity ".

I CON-

I CONSIDER the matter thus.

THE *scripture* is the text. The *creed* is the comment. Now can the comment over-rule the text? Can it alter its original meaning? If not, the text continues still as it was; its original meaning remains still the same. No law can deprive a man of his right of *private judgement* in reference to either. Confequently he is at liberty to form his judgement of both, as shall appear to him to be most consistent with reason and truth.

A LEARNED and conscientious clergy-man coming for institution to a late worthy prelate, took the liberty to ask his lordship, Whether he must be understood by his subscription to resign his judgement in religious concerns to the dictates of authority, and to tie himself down to any other sense of scripture than what should appear to him, upon fair inquiry, to be the true and genuine sense thereof. The Bishop, discerning at once the honest defign of the question, returned this civil and candid answer: "Sir, I have no other concern with your subscription, than to fee that you *do* subscribe. I ask you no questions upon the subject, and

you

you need afk me none. Your liberty, for
Me, remains unaltered and undiminifhed."

THIS was fair and equitable on both
fides. Nor have I the leaft reafon to doubt,
but, that what the bifhop here faid, expreffes upon the whole the united fenfe of
the venerable order of our fuperiors in the
church, concerning fuch matters.

Now laying together, fairly and without
prejudice, thefe feveral confiderations touching the fuperiority of *fcripture* to any human
creeds, or other forms of religious doctrine,
let us apply them briefly to the cafe of fubfcription to any particular articles of the
church of *England*. Suppofe, for inftance,
that of predeftination, or of the defcent
into hades, or any other to which fubfcription is required. To fatisfy myfelf on
this head, I will firft fee what the *fcripture* declares concerning it, fetting down
before me, in one view, and in juft con-
nection, the very words of fcripture, without tacking to them any comment, any expofition, either of my own, or of any other
perfons, in order to accommodate them to
the tenets of any human fyftem. Now
whatever is the true original fenfe of *fcripture* herein, that muft in courfe, and in all
reafon

reafon and equity, be the fenfe in which I
am to fubfcribe the article propofed. Nor
can I, confiftently with my proteftant principles,—with my profeffed fubjection to
Chrift as the fupreme head and lawgiver of
his church, and the fole author and finifher
of my faith,—or with my dutiful acknowledgement of fcripture-authority as fuperior
to all other authority in matters of faith,—
—or with my exprefs declaration to that
purpofe in my fubfcription to the fixth article of the church of *England*, fubfcribe in
any other fenfe whatever [a].

THOSE who may be of a different mind
about thefe matters, I freely permit to enjoy their own fentiments, having no more
to do with *their* confcience and judgement
in fuch things, than they have to do with
mine; which is juft nothing at all. What
I have written, I have written with freedom, on mature reflection, and on a full
perfuafion of the right of private judgement; a privilege which I fhall always
claim, as a Chriftian, and a Proteftant.

OBSERVATIONS

UPON THE FOREGOING SUBJECT.

IT is next to impoſſible for any body of
men, however learned, dignified or diſtinguiſhed, however veſted with public authority, reverenced for their judgement, or
honoured for their elevation, to draw up
ſuch a ſet of articles of religion to be ſubſcribed by the clergy, as will give general
and juſt content, and to which every
thoughtful, judicious and conſcientious
clergyman, having carefully examined and
conſidered them, can readily aſſent and
freely ſubſcribe ; thereby in effect declaring, that thoſe articles do preciſely expreſs
his own ſentiments upon the ſeveral points
therein concluded, and that he believes
they expreſs the very ſenſe of ſcripture on
ſuch heads.

THE reaſons are evident.

1. THE compilers are but men, frail and
fallible, like others of their fellow-beings.

2. THEY

2. THEY commonly accede to the work with their prejudices about them,—their preconceptions in favour of this or that particular tenet or fyftem, to which they have been for fome time devoted. We have a ftrong inftance of this in the account of the *Irifh* articles, drawn up in 1615, by no lefs able and eminent a divine than the moft learned and venerable *Ufher*, the glory of that church, and of the whole republic of letters. He had imbibed early prejudices in favour of fome of the narrow tenets of the great doctor of *Geneva*, and accordingly took the liberty to incorporate into the body of thofe articles the nine decrees of *Lambeth*; which gave juft offence to many learned and judicious men of more enlarged minds. *Keylin's life of Laud*, 194, 195.

3. WHEN the numerous members of a convocation meet together to draw up articles, Are they all of the fame mind with regard to the feveral points to be determined by them? Do they not difcufs thofe queftions over and over, pro and con, before they come (if they come at laft) to a final conclufion? And is it not too well known, how much party and faction generally operate in thofe affemblies, and the prevailing influence of authority and intereft,

tereft, in the event, determines all ? though
many of the members may ftill at the bot-
tom remain diffentients, and could wifh
that matters (fome particulars at leaft) had
been ordered otherwife.

4. If the convocation can be fuppofed
to be thus divided in their fentiments before they come to a conclufion about them,
Can it be fuppofed that the reft of the clergy,
fo concluded in their abfence by the determinations of their fuperiors, would not, if
they had been affembled in the fame convocation, or (which is more feafible) in any
leffer departments and claffes within their
refpective diftricts, have had alfo their different fentiments upon thofe topics, during
the debates about them in thofe affemblies ?
Would they not have declared thefe fentiments openly in the courfe of the debate ?
And would they not afterwards alfo (I mean
after clofing up the final fentence) if they
were left to their liberty, probably do the
fame, expreffing themfelves to the fame purpofe in delivering their mind on each article ? —— How then, it will be afked by
fome, can it well be fuppofed, that fo large a
body of men (not pretending to infpiration) as the whole clergy of *England*,
Ireland, and of feveral extenfive colonies
abroad,

abroad, fhould in a manner all at once become fo unanimous in their opinions and
eonfeffions, touching a great number of articles, as readily to affent to every one of
them, and to teftify that affent by fetting
their hand to them ? And yet fome of thofe
articles are fuppofed, by many learned men,
to be abftrufe enough, and (barring the precluding fentence) ftill difputable.—With the
proper anfwer to this queftion, I have no
concern at prefent, leaving every perfon
concerned to fatisfy his own mind in the
beft manner he can. —— The objeftions
however, now fo current, are ftronger arguments for *dropping* the prefent fubfcriptions altogether, than they are againft in-
dulging a *latitude* of fenfe in fubfcribing.—
The fubfcription (fince it continues to be
impofed) may ftill be rational and confiftent,
if a latitude be allowed. If not allowed
(and do any of our ecclefiaftical governors
difallow it ?) that fame fubfcription may
poffibly, in fome inftances, carry the appearance of fubfcribing to abfurdities, at leaft
to certain tenets that cannot be fufficiently
warranted by fcripture, taken in its original
and true fenfe. — After all, it would furely
be better upon the whole, (as I faid) to put
an end at once to thefe uncandid, though
not always unplaufible objeftions, by put-
ting an end to the *caufes* of Them. —Thefe
confidera-

confiderations fhould no longer be difre-
garded, nor the proper remedies poftponed.
—If much longer poftponed, what will be
the confequences ? *Lector judicet æquus.*

5. Whereas " the avoiding diverfities of
opinions, and eftablifhing confent touching true religion," was at firft the well-
meant defign of fetting up thefe boundaries,
and marking out the precife limits of the
faith which was once delivered to the faints;
unhappy experience hath fince abundantly
convinced all reafonable and obferving men,
that this was a great miftake of our worthy
anceftors ; being a thing that never could
be accomplifhed by any human means ; befides, that it was inconfiftent with the principle of liberty upon which they had fo
lately broke off from the encroachments of
Rome. The principles of liberty are much
better underftood in this age, than they were
in the days of our reformers, when juft reafoning was comparatively but in its infancy.
Later ages have entered deeper into the fubject, ftated it with greater exactnefs, eluci-
dated it in a clearer manner, and corrobo-
rated it with greater force of reafon, than
could have been imagined in the darker
times. No rational man now doubts of
the natural and Chriftian right of private
judgement, which no laws of man can in-
validate.

validate. Judgement is free, and muſt remain ſo.---In ſhort, confidering the general ſtate of the mental frame, and the deſign of Providence in adjuſting it, a ſtrict uniformity in opinion is morally impoſſible, and therefore not to be expected, much leſs to be infiſted upon as neceſſary, or indeed, all circumſtances confidered, as even expedient, towards either the preventing or the terminating of differences about matters of mere opinion or ſpeculation.

To the foregoing remarks we may preſume to add,

6. THAT it may perhaps be ſomewhat queſtioned, and not without reaſon, Whether or how far the authority of any proteſtant church or churches may extend to preſcribe articles, or to decide controverfies, about matters of faith ; or whether, upon the whole, ſuch authority may not either be juſtly thought, or at leaſt ſhrewdly fuſpected, to border ſomewhat too nearly upon that uſurpation of *dominion* over the *faith* and religious liberty of our fellow-chriſtians, which the apoſtles, though divinely inſpired, abſolutely diſclaimed, and our Lord himſelf forbad us to exerciſe, we being all brethren to each other, and fellow-ſervants under Him the ſupreme ruler

I of

of his church, and the fole founder of our faith and religion.

SEVERAL juft objections have been made from time to time, for more than a century paft, to the prefent form of fubfcription, and to more than one or two of the particular objects of it; and much unhappy controverfy hath frequently fubfifted on this fubject.—It may, on many juft and weighty confiderations, be wifhed and requefted, that the terms of fubfcription, hitherto infifted on, were fomewhat moderated, and rendered lefs exceptionable, and lefs difficult to be complied with in certain cafes; efpecially where any honeft and confcientious perfons find themfelves obliged to forbear engaging in our miniftry, on the account of thefe and the like obftacles lying in their way. The relaxation is furely reafonable, and highly defireable; nor is it fo difficult to be accomplifhed, as may by fome be imagined. Prejudice and obftinacy apart, it might, I am perfuaded, be eafily and fafely effected; and the church would be fo far from being a lofer, that fhe would by degrees be a real gainer, by fuch a generous condefcenfion, and juft and equitable indulgence, towards her free-born children.

Suppose a specimen or two should be here submitted to serious and impartial confideration. Possibly some persons who may scruple the present form, may have no objection to the following, or some other of the like import.

I declare myself a Christian *and a* Protestant. *I believe and assert that the holy* Scriptures *of the old and new Testament (as acknowledged and referred to in the sixth article of the church of* England*) contains the whole will of God relating to the salvation of man, through Christ Jesus; and will make those* Scriptures *the rule and foundation of my instructions and exhortations to those who shall be committed to my ministerial charge: Nor will I teach any other doctrine, either in public or in private, but what I am and shall be persuaded to be the will and doctrine of God therein contained.* **A. B.**

Or : .

I do here profess and declare my sincere and firm belief in One God, the Creator, Preserver and Governor of the world: And in Jesus Christ *the Son of God and Saviour of the world: And in the Holy Spirit of God and of Christ, as described in the Scriptures. I believe*

lieve

lieve the divine authority of the Scriptures, *as generally received among Christians; and their sufficiency for salvation through faith in Christ. I believe the necessity of a godly, righteous and sober life, and its acceptableness with God to salvation through him. I believe all things revealed in the* Scriptures *for that end;—the mediation of Christ, the aids of his spirit, the resurrection of the dead, the general judgement, and the future state of rewards and punishments. I renounce all authority in matters of faith beside that of the* Scriptures *; and do promise that I will carefully study those* Scriptures, *and that I will teach and preach no other doctrine or doctrines as necessary to salvation, but what I am and shall be persuaded to be agreeable to the* Scriptures, *and to express the true meaning and design thereof.* A. B.

Suppose now, it should be left to the *choice* of candidates for orders, and of those who apply for institution into benefices, to subscribe either the one or the other of these or the like forms before their admission; such a subscription might reasonably be judged sufficient to answer any or all useful purposes for which the present forms can be supposed to be designed, or can indeed possibly accomplish, without infringing the rule of moral equity, and doing

injury

injury to the juft claims of rational and Chriftian liberty: which liberty fhould never be curtailed in any points of mo- ment, and which a ftrict impofition of problematical opinions hath always incommoded, and ever will incommode, and perhaps at laft totally deftroy.

If thefe or the like tefts, tho' really in themfelves fufficient to anfwer all the reafonable purpofes of fubfcription in any truly proteftant church, fhould after all be deemed infufficient, or thought to fall fhort of the end in view; all I can fay farther. is, that to prevent all future differences on this head, and to fecure the peace of the ftate, in reference to fuch matters, a fet of well-compofed *Homilies*, upon the plaineft and moft neceffary fubjects of religion, and the beft adapted for general inftruction and. common benefit, may be enjoined and authorifed by the ftate, to be diftinctly and folemnly pronounced, in regular order, from year to year, by the ftated minifter or minifters, in all churches and chapels throughout the realm. Such a provifion and injunction, preferable at leaft to the prefent touching fubfcription, might upon the whole be of confiderable fervice to the community, and contribute in a good degree to prevent or moderate litigations on this

I 3   head,

head, and other topics of religion, which are so often detrimental to the public tranquility.

I DESIRE it may be noted, that what is here proposed concerning *Homilies*, is principally intended to obviate an objection that may be suggested against discontinuing the present forms of subscription to articles; and is by no means intended to preclude, or in the least to interfere with, the most useful and necessary duty of *preaching*; a duty of divine institution, and not to be dispensed with by any human authority. Wise and good men, true ministers of Christ, having made the proper declaration and subscription, as above proposed, will always keep within their just bounds, being careful to observe their engagements, and do honour to their function; and may safely be entrusted with the discharge of the important office of *preaching*.

NOR will this liberty render the use of the *homilies* needless. They may still be kept up, and publicly read as proposed, every year, to the no small benefit of christian auditories, especially the more illiterate part of them, who greatly stand in need of such plain instructions, and for whose improvement in Christian knowledge

4

and practice such popular discourses ought to be chiefly calculated.

A NOBLE collection of this kind might be made (if made with true judgement, and without intermixing any points of doubtful disputation) out of the best *English* sermons already extant : And such a collection would do real honour to this church and nation, and particularly to the clergy; exhibiting such illustrious examples in this kind to other protestant churches, if not also to that of *Rome.*

IF any clergymen, after subscription (as before supposed) shall make *undue use* of the liberty of preaching, and persist to misapply that liberty, the state, after having given due admonition, may very justly, either totally prohibit their preaching, or, which may on some accounts be better, confine them to the use of the homilies only ; as they may also, for a while confine young divines, not as yet sufficiently exercised in the word and ministry, and less acquainted with the true design of preaching the gospel of Christ to the world. Which is not to acquire temporary lucre here, but to prepare men for life and immortality hereafter.

I 4

N.

Candid *sentiments in favour of dutiful applications for a review.*

CANDOUR, benevolence, and generosity of temper, joined with good sense and solid judgement, will always incline men to judge favourably of any well meant attempt, conducted with moderation, to serve the interest of true religion, and promote the honour of the *English* reformation.

SEVERAL endeavours of this kind have been exerted of late years, and been well received and approved by men of serious piety, unbiassed in their affections, and unprejudiced in their inquiries: who well understood the Christian religion, and wished to see many things in the church of *England* rectified, according to the model of that religion; being well-known friends to

this

this church, and men who underſtand, and would promote its true intereſt.

SOME indeed have ſtood out in oppoſition to theſe benevolent undertakings, and done what they could to prevent the good ſuccefs of them. The motives to this oppoſition are ſufficiently obvious, and ſcarce any one that has any tolerable knowledge of the world, and the ſelf-intereſted views of many men in it (regardlefs, in compariſon, of the intereſts of true Chriſtianity,) can fail of gueſſing aright concerning the hidden ſprings of theſe perverſe proceedings.

OTHER things in the writings of this prejudiced ſet of men, may be borne with ; but bitterneſs and virulence (the common ef- fects of church-bigotry) are inexcuſable— With how much better ſpirit, better ſenſe, and better judgement, does a moſt learned and worthy perſon (now deſervedly exalted to one of the higheſt ſtations in the church) ſpeak of all good endeavours tending to the improvement of it, and calculated for the advancement of true religion in it : Enough one would think, to excite at leaſt ſome little diffidence, and even of regret and ſelf- condemnation, in thoſe who have hitherto been ſo peremptory and aſſuming, and, not unfrequently, contemptuous and overbearing,

ing, in their treatment of their brethren on
thefe and the like occafions.

" LET no one lightly entertain fufpicions
of any ferious propofal for the advancement of religious knowledge; nor out of
unreafonable prejudice endeavour to obftruct
any inquiry, that profeffes to aim at the farther illuftration of the great fcheme of the
gofpel in general, or the removal of error in
any part, in faith, in doctrine, in practice,
or in worfhip." Dr. *Lowth*'s vifitation-fer-
mon at *Durham*, 1758, publifhed at the re-
queft of the Lord Bifhop of that diocefe.

ANOTHER well-tempered and judicious
divine of our eftablifhment, having obferved
the indifcreet conduct and malevolent fpirit
of fome men, in oppofing all good defigns
for farther reformation and improvement in
this church, thus delivers his thoughts with
moderation and reafon.

" SOME few things in our eftablifhed
mode of worfhip and difcipline have been
thought capable of being better adapted to
the defign of Chriftianity, and reprefenta-
tions have been made from time to time,
propofing to bring thefe things to a maturer
and more accurate revifal. Such reprefen-
tations, it is true, have been too often made
with an indecent acrimony of ftyle, and
ground-

groundlefs invectives againft the prefent fpirit of the church itfelf, and the faireft characters that have ever adorned it. To thefe,
the moft effectual anfwer would be an example of greater moderation and candour
in ourfelves. We have indeed no other way
of confuting this calumny, but by evidenc-
ing the fame principles now, which origi-
nally gave rife to our happy conftitution;
by our general readinefs to embrace the
truth, in what garb, and from what quar-
ter foever it may chance to be conveyed to
us, by our free acknowledgement upon conviction, fhould there appear to be a real
expediency for fuch a revifal, and confiftently with this conviction, by our unanimous concurrence in every prudent endeavour, and feafonable application to procure
it. —— Should the candid and refpectful
difquifitions of fincere and hearty well-
wifhers to our eftablifhment, upon the pof-
fibility of raifing it a fingle ftep nearer to
perfection, be reprefented as tending not
to improve, to ftrengthen and perpetuate
it, but to overturn and ruin it altogether;
will it not be faid, that very flender indeed
is our efteem of the folidity, or fundamental
right conftruction of the fabric itfelf, if we
fufpect its ability to ftand a flight examination? But if it fhall appear that we caft
them afide with contempt, or anfwer them
only

only with illiberal abuſe, an overbearing,
method of diſputation, and every little art,
of evading and perplexing the point in debate, will not our adverſaries be ready to
remind us of the ſimilar conduct of the
Scribes and Phariſees of old, and the ſeve-
rity of the cenſure paſſed upon them by
truth and righteouſneſs itſelf? How cheap
a triumph ſhall we thus afford them, by
injudiciouſly ſtooping to the ſame low ſhifts
in defence of a better cauſe! Let us rather
openly ſhew that we fear no conſequences
of bringing our excellent eſtabliſhment to
the ſtricteſt ſcrutiny, by chearfully uniting
our endeavours, our good wiſhes at leaſt,
for that purpoſe, with thoſe of every decent and fair diſquiſitor, never doubting but
its own intrinſic merit upon the whole, will
of itſelf protect from injury every eſſential
and important part of it.

—— "All human regulations without
exemption are amenable to the bar of reaſon.
They may claim obedience, it is true, from
every member of a community, as far as
they are conſiſtent with the laws of God.
Notwithſtanding this, whatever natural
rights men may in a ſocial ſtate be reaſonably led or compelled to ſurrender, their
right of *private judgement* muſt remain for
ever unalienable, as well with reſpect to eccleſiaſtical

clefiaftical as to civil regulations. Decently
to remonftrate againft any inconvenience
apprehended to arife from human laws of
either fort, fhould by no means be deemed
incompatible with all the deference that is
due to the authority of their fuperiors ; all
the requifite obfervance being in the mean
time dutifully fubmitted to, and all juft
acknowledgements humbly paid to the good
intentions of the impofers. Inftead of re-
fenting this conduct as an infult againft an
eftablifhment founded on religious liberty,
let us be affured that its moft venerable
guardians regard it rather as a teftimony of
a fincere efteem of their judgement and
candour, as proceeding from a real perfuafion, that they confider their exalted
ftation as an engagement to diftinguifh
themfelves in fupport of the principles of
true proteftantifm.—In fact, no offence is
likely to be taken by thofe, who are principally concerned to declare it, at any attempt conducted with the fame fpirit, to
ftrike out from the moft harmonious and
complete conftitution, every occafion of
difcord, every fhadow of an imperfection."
Dr. *Duncan's* fermon at the Bifhop of
Winchefter's annual vifitation at *Bafingftoke,*
1769. In p. 22, is a proper note [14] refer-
ring to Dr. *Balguy's* fermon at the confecration of the Bifhop of *Landaff.*

SOME

SOME controverted doctrines contained in the *articles* of the church, " have been interpreted in a different sense by writers of the first authority in the church. This *latitude* of construction seems to have been claimed and allowed from the beginning. It has been defended by almost all who have written professedly upon them; and they have certainly, for more than a century past, been generally interpreted, and that openly and avowedly, and therefore, I hope honestly, with this latitude. But it is still pain and grief to ingenuous minds to *subscribe* to forms, which in their first appearance they cannot approve. I must therefore earnestly join with those who wish to see the ministers of our church relieved from this burden : from which, though bound by the same law, and formerly attached, at least as firmly by prejudice, to the rigid interpretation, the ministers of our dissenting churches have found a way, and are, I am informed, very generally allowed by their congregations, as well as by the magistrate, to exempt themselves. That there have been, and may still subsist, many difficulties in the way of attempting this alteration in our national church, every thinking and candid person will allow. And therefore, till this

can

can be done, it feems a duty in all to forbear complaining of their fuperiors, and
fo judge charitably of thofe, who, in fubfcribing the fame forms, affume a liberty
of differing from them in the manner of
interpretation : and for which licence they
may now furely plead the tacit confent
and allowance both of the church and
ftate." Dr. *Adams*'s fermon intitled *A teſt
of true and falfe doctrines,* preached at *Sa-
lop,* 1769.—Concerning the dropping of
fubfcriptions in feveral proteftant congregations in *England* [25], fee *Remarks on the fecond and third letters againſt the Confeſſional,*
1768, p. 28.

Some farther remarks on the fame fubject.

DR. *Adams*'s obfervation is a very juſt
one, that tho' the articles are now generally interpreted with a *latitude,* and that,
without any apparent difapprobation on the
part of the governors, ftill it is *pain and
grief to ingenuous minds to* fubfcribe *to forms,
which in their firſt appearance they cannot
approve.* Is the continuing to enjoin this
practice, either fo defireable and neceffary
on the part of the governors, that it cannot be difpenfed with ; or fo agreeable and
convenient on that of the governed, that
they will be loath to give up a cuftom en-
tailed

tailed upon them by their venerable an-
ceſtors ? Will it not be thought that the
conduct of the former, may have too much
in it of the appearance of uſurping dominion over conſcience, and that the conduct of the latter may ſeem to carry
ſome reſemblance of practiſing the long ex-
ploded doctrine of *paſſive obedience ?* The
ſituation of the latter in this reſpect, ſeems
to be by no means eligible ; and it may
well be hoped, that it is in the power of
the former to relieve their brethren under
theſe difficulties ²⁶. It cannot ſurely be
ſuppoſed that the Apoſtles, if they were
ſtill living, would lay upon them ſuch
burdens; nor can it reaſonably be imagined, that ſince this practice is found to
be now exiſting, being enjoined and enforced by mere human authority, they would
commend goſpel-miniſters for ſo tamely
giving up their goſpel-liberty, and much
leſs if thereby they brought their conſciences into a ſnare, and departed in any degree from the integrity and ſimplicity of
the Chriſtian character. When *Peter* de-
baſed himſelf by criminal compliances, in-
conſiſtent with that character, in order to
ingratiate himſelf with a prevailing ſect,
St. *Paul*, we are told, withſtood him to
the face, and cogently remonſtrated againſt
thoſe compliances, as unſuitable to the
profeſſion

profeſſion of a Chriſtian, and much more
of a Chriſtian miniſter, whoſe principal
care and concern it ſhould be, that the mi-
niſtry might not by his miſconduct be juſtly
blamed.   Where the Apoſtle plainly inti-
mates the neceſſity of being upon guard
againſt temptation, and every inducement
to offend conſcience. No political motives,
no prudential conſiderations, no worldly intereſts, ſhould induce us to act inconſiſtent-
ly with known duty.

AND beſides, we ought to pay ſome decent regard to the ſentiments of the *world*
concerning our conduct in this matter.
For, however we may ſatisfy ourſelves,
whether upon principles of expedience and
preſent intereſt, or thoſe of any more laudable nature, the world will generally entertain but an indifferent opinion of our integrity in our ſubſcriptions, and will impute them to other motives than a perſua-
ſion of the truth of what we ſubſcribe to.
Severe have been the cenſures, and frequent
the charges, thrown out againſt the clergy
in this view.   Churchmen, as they would
ſtill be thought, have joined with unbelievers in the cry; which is now become
a common topic of converſation and of
pamphlets, and leſſens the eſteem of the
clergy among the people. A very keen
unbeliever ſpeaks with great contempt both

K   of

of them and of their fubfcriptions:—"Thofe
dirty fences, fays he, of the church called
fubfcriptions; which are not only the ftain
of a good confcience, but difcouragements
· in the ftudy of the fcriptures," [how little
foever he regarded thofe fcriptures.] And
again, he charges the clergy as being in
thefe and the like refpects a very bad fort
of men, paying little or no regard to honour and confcience, integrity and truth,
when their intereft comes in competition
with either. " The clergy, he fays, in
their principles, in their oaths, and in their
fubfcriptions, are fo accuftomed to *prevari-*
cate with God and man !"—The other clafs
of objectors, no lefs virulent, and of the
two more heated with zeal, fpeak of this
reverend fraternity as a fet of men, " who
have impioufly and hypocritically fet their
hands to doctrines, which in their hearts
they never affented to,—carrying on a folemn farce of fubfcribing," &c. Again :
" Religion (they obferve) is fadly expofed
and brought into contempt, by the conduct
of too many of the clergy, in fubfcribing
to what they do not believe, and fubmitting to the loweft and bafeft equivocations
in order to defend proceedings, which in
every other fphere of life would be condemned as contrary to all the received
principles of common honefty and fair dealing amongft men." And the objectors cor-
roborate

roborate their obfervations with thofe noted words of Dr. *Waterland*; " If either ftate-oaths on the one hand, or church-fubfcriptions on the other, once come to be made light of, and fubtleties be invented to defend or palliate fuch grofs infincerity ; we may bid farewell to principles, and religion will be little elfe but difguifed atheifm." —Serious men will allow, that thefe words carry weight with them, and deferve to be regarded ; and zealots will not fail to turn them into obloquies and reproaches. Now,

Can we hear thefe obloquies, and bear with thefe reproaches from year to year, without concern, without emotion, without any endeavours to cut off the occafion of them ; which is fo obvious to every one's view, and cannot be denied to be prejudicial to the intereft of religion, as it brings fuch fevere reflections upon the teachers of it.

For my own part, I am fully convinced, that thefe and the like reflections will always be flung out againft the clergy of the church of *England*, fo long as they are tied down by their governors to the neceffity of fubfcribing to human forms ; which are, fome of them at leaft, of dubious interpretation, if not alfo of dubious authority, and are

K 2   and

and will always be a means of perpetuating debate and contention (inftead of *eftablifhing confent touching true religion)* among his Majefty's fubjects in thefe kingdoms. And are debates and contentions fuch defireable things among fellow-chriftians, fellow-pro-teftants, and fellow-fubjects under the fame government ? The intereft of our country in church and ftate, calls for commifera-tion, calls for redrefs in this matter : a fa-vour which it may be hoped will not be much longer delayed. The occafions are preffing, the diforders menacing, and pro-bably will be growing, till a redrefs is granted. Which, as far as hitherto ap-pears, can no other way be accomplifhed, than by dropping the prefent forms of fub-fcription altogether, and contriving fome other and better method, which is fuffici-ently feafible, of fecuring a fet of faithful minifters to the church, and reftoring peace to it [17].

4

THE

THE

EDITOR's REMARKS

On N° I.

1 *A* N D, *in effect, the text into the bar-gain.*] The text is *Heb.* xiii. 17. *Obey them that have the rule over you, and submit yourselves; for they watch for your souls.*—Of the numerous obstacles which are found in the way of scripture-knowledge, there is scarce any one we have greater reason to lament, than the supineness with which so many are observed to rely on the judgement of commentators, to the distrust or neglect of their own understandings. " It has never been doubted," says Dr. *Balguy*, " that the authority of which " the Apostle here speaks, is *Church*-autho-" rity." Perhaps we should find, were we to make the search, that the doctor is under a mistake in supposing this has *never* been doubted. But if we should not, yet the suffrage of the whole tribe of expositors ought not to have had any weight, where so

K 3   little

little befide appeared to countenancè fuch
an interpretation.

THAT the Apoftle fpeaks here of
church-authority, "*fufficiently* appears," it
is faid, " from the reafon affigned for our
" fubjection. We are to obey our gover-
" nors, becaufe they watch *for our fouls:*
" a circumftance which clearly points out
" fpiritual authority, and diftinguifhes it
" from civil."—This is a moft trivial circumftance indeed, and which one is furprifed to find a man of Dr. *Balguy's* erudition, laying fo great a ftrefs upon. From
the mere *Englifh* reader alone fuch an obfervation might be expected. So then it
fhould feem, that if it had been rendered
—"*for they watch for* YOU"—inftead of, *for*
" YOUR SOULS"—the objects of that obedience and fubjection which the Apoftle re-
commends, might be our *civil* governors ;
at leaft, *fpiritual* authority would not have
been " clearly pointed out." And can the
doctor be ignorant, that ψυχη is frequently
ufed by the facred writers for the *whole*
perfon?—To mention no other inftance, it
is fo ufed in *Rom.* xiii. 1. and that on the
very fubject of obedience and fubmiffion to
civil authority. " *Let every* SOUL (ψυχη)
" [every perfon] *be fubject to the higher*
" *powers.*"

WE

WE may obferve alfo, that the circumftance in the text under confideration, which
is fuppofed fo clearly to point out fpiritual
authority, *viz.* " *they watch for your fouls*"
—depends upon an *uncertain* rendering of
the original. If the comma after υμων had
been placed after the word αγρυπνουσιν, the
rendering muft not have been " they *watch*
" *for your fouls*"—but, " they watch, as
" they that muft give an account *for your*
" *fouls*"—[of or concerning you.] And
this punctuation is both admiffible on gram-
matical principles, and conformable alfo to
the reading of the *Alexandrine Copy* itfelf,
which puts υπερ των ψυχων υμων after the
word αποδωσοντες. This, however, is not
mentioned in preference to the reading
which our tranflators followed; but only
to fhew on how uncertain a foundation
Dr. *Balguy*'s whole fyftem muft reft, who
could confider a circumftance fo frivolous
and dubious, as " *clearly* and *fufficiently*
" pointing out fpiritual authority, and dif-
" tinguifhing it from civil."

AGAINST this *only* circumftance in the
text, and the authority of expofitors, which
to our aftonifhment have appeared decifive
to the learned writer, it will be fufficient to
weigh the general tenor of the inftructions
of

of Chriſt, and his apoſtles on the head of ſubjeċtion to human authority. In matters of
a *civil* and merely temporal concern, obedience and ſubjeċtion thereto are frequently
enjoined ; in thoſe of a *ſpiritual* nature, they
are not only *unenjoined,* but abſolutely *forbidden.* In *theſe,* to Jeſus Chriſt *alone* is
obedience ever repreſented as due. Even his
own miniſters, the apoſtles, who aċted under his immediate *commiſſion,* claimed it not
to themſelves.

YET there are not wanting directions
to Chriſtians, reſpeċting their duty towards
their ſpiritual inſtruċtors. At the ſeventh
verſe of this very chapter from which the
Doċtor has choſen the ſubjeċt of his diſcourſe,
we meet with two direċtions on this head.
But neither of them point out *obedience* and
ſubjeċtion to be the due of ſuch rulers as
are there referred to. " REMEMBER *them*
" *which have the rule over you, who have*
" *ſpoken unto you the word of God : whoſe*
" FAITH FOLLOW, *conſidering the end of*
" *their converſation."* Theſe faithful diſ-
penſers of the word of God were well worthy of kind *remembrance* and a careful *imitation* from their hearers, whoſe *maſters,*
however, they were not, that they ſhould
be *obeyed.* But the rulers referred to in the
17th verſe are conſidered by the apoſtle as
entitled

entitled to *obedience* and *fubmiſſion*; a circumſtance which clearly points out civil authority, and diſtinguiſhes it from ſpiritual.
Nor is the reaſon aſſigned for our ſubjec-
tion incompatible with the ſuppoſition, that
the apoſtle ſpeaks here of civil authority.
On the contrary, it is aſſigned with great
conſiſtency and propriety. We are to obey
our civil governors, becauſe they *watch for*
[υπερ, over] *us, as they that muſt give an account*; that is, thoſe who are placed in authority over us exerciſe that authority in
our own behalf. It is to our advantage and
not detriment, that they are entruſted with
it; and they are bound to uſe it to this end,
being themſelves under authority, and having their ſuperiors in the ſtate to whom they
are accountable for the diſcharge of their
office in the protection and ſecurity of our
perſons and properties : Or, it may be, the
apoſtle refers here to the care theſe rulers
were appointed by the ſtate to exerciſe more
particularly over *Chriſtians*, to obſerve and
inſpect narrowly their conduct, to watch
and *keep guard*, αγρυπνουσιν, over this new
ſect, whoſe behaviour they were to report
to the higher powers, and were anſwerable
for any diſturbance they might occaſion,
and mal-practices they might be guilty of
againſt the ſtate. But in whichever of theſe
two ways we may underſtand the reaſon
                                        aſſigned

affigned by the apoftle for the obedience
and fubmiffion of thofe to whom he writes,
it is far from being inapplicable to his defign
of admonifhing them of the duty they owe
to their *civil* governors.

* *Either church.*] How could our author expect to find Dr. *Balguy*'s defcription
of a Church in agreement with any of the
defcriptions given of a *Chriftian* church ?—
The doctor acknowledges, that in what he
hath faid of church-authority he hath confidered a church, as an inftitution *merely
human.* Neither the Chriftian church in
general, therefore, nor a Chriftian church
in particular, was neceffary to be defcribed.
The marks and characters of either would
only have encumbered his plan, and ferved
to expofe its *heterogeneous* mixture.

³ *A circumftance of no moment.*] The
paffage in Dr. *Balguy*'s fermon here referred
to ftands thus — " It will be urged, per-
" haps, that I have confidered a Church
" as an inftitution merely *human ;* whereas
" the *Chriftian* church derives its authority
" from God.—This will be readily admit-
" ted : but the Divinity of its origin is a
" circumftance of *no moment* in the pre-
" fent enquiry." True ; this circumftance
is

is of no moment in the *prefent enquiry*; that is to fay, as it is conducted by the Preacher. But then another objection lies againft all that has been urged in the fermon; which is, that the *prefent enquiry* is itfelf of *no moment* to the church of *England*, as part of the *Chriftian* church. We want not to know our rights and duties in our merely civil and political capacities, what fubmif-fion is due to them *that have the rule over us*, and what rights belong to them, confi-dered as prefiding over a *merely human* in-ftitution; but in what relation the church and its governors ftand to each other, con-fidered, both of them, as members of the *Chriftian* church, and acknowledging the *Divine* original and authority of fcripture. The enquiry, purfued without any regard to this circumftance, concerns us not as *Chriftians*, but as *fubjects*; and is, in fact, an enquiry into the nature and extent of *civil* and *political* authority, not of *fpiritual*, to which, however, the archdeacon fuppofeth his text to refer, and in refpect of which he propofed to give, in his difcourfe, *an ac-curate defcription of our rights and duties*, in vain, he tells us, fought for in fcripture it-felf.

4 *Every form of religion, &c.*] In mak-ing this extract, our author has wanted his
ufual

ufual accuracy. This is obferved in juftice
to Dr. *Balguy*, who doth not *affert*, that
" every form of religion requires attention
" and ftudy in thofe who are to teach it."
He is fpeaking of the advantages which
may be obtained by committing the offices
of religion to fome certain perfons. Among
other advantages attending a defignation of
particular perfons, is mentioned the following one, *viz.* that " they [the offices]
" are much more likely to be performed as
" they *ought* to be. This at leaft," it is
added, " muft be true *under every form of*
" *religion*, that *requires* attention and ftudy
" in thofe who are to teach it."

5 *Nor will he give, &c.*] Dr. *Balguy*'s
words are—" *No* man *will* give his time to
" the public, unlefs excited by public re-
" wards: No man *can* give his *whole* time,
" without expofing himfelf to want and
" ruin."—It is not to be doubted, however, that in the firft ages of Chriftianity
many men gave their time, and no fmall
portion of it too, to the public for this valuable purpofe, *unexcited* thereto by public
rewards. Nor are we without inftances,
in thefe latter times, of our religion being
moft ably defended, its doctrines rationally
explained, and its precepts warmly and for-
cibly recommended by men who were in-
fluenced

fluenced by no mercenary views, who for
their valuable labours of this kind, neither
enjoyed any public emoluments, nor entertained expectations of any other rewards
than thofe which accompany willing and
gratuitous endeavours to ferve the caufe of
true religion. The reader will anticipate
fome of the following names, fo juftly celebrated, and all worthy to be mentioned and
remembered with efteem—*Locke*, Sir *Ifaac
Newton*, Sir *Peter King*, *Milton*, *Addifon*,
Steel, *Littleton*, *Weft*, *Collet*.

‘ *Confiftent and uniform*.] It is really
aftonifhing how weakly, and how difcredi-
tably for the proteftant caufe, this fame outward confiftency and uniformity in religion
is praifed and pleaded for by the modern
advocates for church-authority. Here it is
recommended as being, of the *higheft* importance to the interefts of religion. Surely
our preacher would do well to confider,
that religion was *moft* confiftent and uniform
in its outward appearance, when its native
influence on the underftandings and hearts
of men was *moft* obftructed by the corrup-
tions of the church of *Rome*. *External* uniformity in religious worfhip, fo much the
boaft of that church, is, and can only be,
the effect of an *implicit* obedience to human
authority. Where the right to private
judgement

judgement is afferted, and while men continue to be men, that is to fay, fallible beings, religion in its outward appearance
will not be uniform. It was the affertion
of this right which broke the *uniformity* of
the church at the reformation, and has introduced fuch a *variety* of external modes
of worfhip. Yet, which is of the *higheft* importance to the *real* interefts of religion ;
uniformity in its outward appearance, (which
impofition on the confciences of men can
alone effect) or the exercife of private judgement, (which admits not of fuch an uniformity) can be no queftion with a confiftent
proteftant.

But " without uniformity," fays the
Doctor, " public inftitutions can never ob-
" tain their full effect." *Public inftitu-*
tions are here ambiguoufly ufed. But will
it be affirmed, that the religion *publicly in-*
ftituted by Chrift and his apoftles may not
have its genuine effect upon the minds and
conduct of its profeffors, without this *ex-*
ternal uniformity ? — Surely not.

It is further urged, in behalf of uniformity, that " doubt and difcord are the
" inevitable confequences of *diffenfion*." If
by *diffenfion* is meant (what fhould be meant
in this place) want of uniformity, nothing
                                                    can

can be lefs true than the above affertion.
Perfons may chufe to be *uniform* in the outward appearance of religion, who yet may
entertain much *doubt* of the truth and ex-
cellency of the doctrines they profefs. But
fo far is doubt from being an inevitable
confequence of diffent from the mode of religion eftablifhed in any community, that
it is generally the *caufe* of that diffent. Nor
is it more true that *difcord* is an inevitable
confequence of the want of external uniformity in religion : The papifts excepted, who
of all thofe that diffent from the mode of religious worfhip eftablifhed in this country,
are, in *confequence* of that diffent, the more
troublefome and factious members of the
community.—Nay, difcord and diffenfion,
it is but too well known, have been the *confequence* of attempting to enforce this fame
uniformity in the outward appearance of religion; and concord and unanimity have
been happily experienced to refult from
every act of indulgence fhewn to *proteftants*
in the exercife of their various modes of
religious worfhip.

" EITHER," the Doctor further obferves,
" the variety of religious forms, fhakes and
" fubverts the belief of all religion ; or the
" warmth of oppofition, whilft it kindles
" mens zeal, fuppreffes and ftifles every
" other

" other virtue."—On the former of thefe obfervations it will be fufficient to remark, that there is not the leaft proof here adduced of the effect attributed to this variety in the outward appearance of religion. And the probability is on the other hand; *viz.* that the permitting the members of any community to worfhip God—every fect in its own way—will not fhake and fubvert the belief of *all* religion, but rather tend to promote and confirm the *true*, while it is a trial indeed upon *all* religion. As to the latter obfervation, that " the warmth of " oppofition fuppreffes and ftifles every vir- " tue," if it be a juft one, is it not the ftrongeft argument poffible againft rigoroufly infifting upon an external uniformity in religion?—For, *this* it is which caufeth that warmth of oppofition complained of. While every fect enjoys, and is protected by government in the exercife of its own mode of worfhip, there is no foundation for oppofition: And in that cafe, if " mens " zeal be kindled," it can exert itfelf in no way that will be prejudicial to the interefts of religion and morality, or troublefome to civil government.—See this fubject more largely difcuffed in anfwer to Letters concerning Confeffions of Faith, *&c.* Part iii. p. 9—26. *Newbery,* 1769.

⁷ —*All church-authority should be under the controul of the civil governor.*] It is the duty of the civil governor, not only himself to forbear exercising any dominion over conscience, but also to protect his subjects from the attempts of others to lord it over their consciences. For this end alone, *viz.* the protection of the subject against any unjust claims of church-authority, it is that church-authority should be under the controul of the civil governor. But then the civil governor, who is to frame his public conduct by the laws of the community, should himself be under the controul of *such* laws as are calculated to support, not to infringe the rights of conscience: In other words, conscience ought not to be under the controul of either our *civil,* or *ecclesiastical* governors ; it should be perfectly *free,* and that freedom secured to every member of the community by *law.*

⁸ *Not the* BEST *but the* LARGEST *sect will naturally demand the protection of the magistrate.*] But why should not *both* of them receive the protection of the magistrate ?—If the *largest* " will naturally demand" it, the *best* will surely *deserve* it. And should not *merit* weigh more with the magistrate, than *numbers ?*— To speak the

L　　　　　　　plain

plain truth, Dr. *Balguy* ought to be afhamed of the principle on which he limits the protection of the magiftrate. Not only is the *beft*, equally with the *largeft fect*, entitled thereto, but every *individual* hath a *natural* and unalienable right to the fame.

⁹ *That authority once* ESTABLISHED *muft be* OBEYED.] If this be true, how fhall we vindicate the reformation from popery?—The authority of the church of *Rome* was once eftablifhed in thefe kingdoms. Ought it to have been *obeyed?* — It ought; and " thofe that refifted it, refifted the ordi-" nance of God, and received unto them-" felves damnation," *if* what the Doctor alledges be true, that the founders of our religion are in this one point clear and explicit, that authority once *eftablifhed* muft be *obeyed*. But it is *not* true; fo far from it, that in this one point, *viz.* of fubjection to human authority in the matter of religion, the founder of our faith is clear and explicit, that fuch authority ought neither to be *eftablifhed* nor *obeyed*. " Be not ye called Rabbi: for one " is your mafter, even Chrift, and all ye " are brethren. And call no man your fa-" ther upon the earth: for one is your fa-" ther which is in heaven."

¹⁰ *An unbeliever in* MANY *of thofe arti-cles.*]

cles.] Why should Dr. *Balguy* lye under this imputation?—Who has any business with his sincerity or insincerity in subscribing the 39 articles?—This concerns *himself* greatly; but it concerns himself *only.* " I " would not myself," says our author, " af- " firm this," [that the doctor is a *non-be- lieving* subscriber.] No : That would have been very unlike our author's candid turn of mind, as well as the decency and good manners with which *his own* remarks are always made. Yet I cannot help wishing he had forborne to suggest the suspicion of any *other* person on this head. And upon what does the writer here cited ground his charge? Why truly, upon his own opinion of Dr. *Balguy's* good sense. " I have," saith he, " so " good an opinion of Dr. *Balguy's* good sense, " as to think it is a thousand to one, but " that he himself is an unbeliever in *many* " of those articles." How weak!—How arrogant!—Has the archdeacon actually expressed any dissatisfaction with the articles to which he has subscribed?—Has he betrayed any symptoms of the insincerity of which he is here accused, by any refinement upon the nature and end of subscription, or by a forced and ambiguous construction of any particular articles?—If he has, his *considerer* would not have done amiss, nor taken an unjustifiable liberty with

L 2   him,

him, in pointing out the inftances. But nothing of this kind appears in the fermon. It is the preacher's *good fenfe* only which makes this vaft odds of a *thoufand to one* againft his honefty in fubfcribing. In fhort, this writer fits in judgement upon Dr. *Balguy* and the *Englifh* clergy in general, with the like felf-fufficiency that deifts and infidels ufually exhibit in judging the profeffors of Chriftianity. Poffeffed of great *good fenfe* themfelves, and meafuring other men's underftandings by their own, with *them* it is a *thoufand to one* but that every man of *good fenfe* is an unbeliever in *many* articles of that religion.

REMARKS

On N° II.

" *One third of the* 39 *Articles of the church of England ?*—] A moft invidious queftion this indeed! But I am perfuaded the heavy charge againft the clergy of the church of *England*, which it implies, and is meant to fet forth, will hurt our accufer, on a *juft* reflection upon it, much more than we may fuffer in the efteem of *candid* men, through any credit that will be given

to

to his representation. Dr. *Priestley* has an undoubted right to *his own thoughts* of the established clergy, and the system of faith and doctrine to which they are required to subscribe. To point out too, and expose any defects in the latter, and to admonish, and expostulate with any of the former, who may stand *convicted* of certain gross inconsistencies with the solemn profession they made at the time of subscribing, is not any unjustifiable liberty. For this may be done with candour, with decency, and with some advantage to the cause of truth and reformation. But to charge us (at least, to insinuate such a charge) with *not believing*, if we read and think *at all, one third* of what we have solemnly subscribed, is more than uncandid and indecent; it is to de-tract from our good name; it is to judge us too in a matter on which *man*'s judgement ought not to be given. We are more-over, from the very nature of such a charge, precluded from pleading to it, though we may be perfectly innocent. Conscience may acquit us of insincerity to *ourselves*, but it cannot be *produced* in evidence of our sin-cerity.

If Dr. *Priestley* had expressed only *his own* thoughts of us in this place, and told us that *he* " supposed us not to believe one

" third

" third of the 39 articles," *uncandid* and *illiberal* still he must have been accounted, but clear of the *injustice* of representing the generality of dissenters as harbouring the like uncharitable opinion of us. — *" Who " among the clergy, that read and think at " all, are supposed to believe one third of the " thirty-nine articles of the church of Eng- " land?"*—Questions of this kind are not asked for the sake of information. But I shall leave the doctor to pick out what information he can on the subject from the two following extracts from a pamphlet *; which I have perused with great pleasure; and which fully proves, that freedom of sentiment in religion, and of speech also, is perfectly consistent with a regard to decency in remarking upon the establishment, and judging its professors.

Mr. *Taylor*, being asked at his ordination, *his opinion of the dissenting interest, and his reasons for engaging in the ministry among the dissenters*, to his opinion freely given adds — " But though I profess myself a

---

* The Duties of religious societies considered, in a sermon preached at the ordination of the Rev. PHILIP TAYLOR, at *Liverpool*, *June* 21st—And of the Rev. ROBERT GORE, at *Manchester*, *August* 23d, 1770. By the Rev. WILLIAM ENFIELD; with an ADDRESS, &c. *London* : Printed for *J. Johnson*, 1770.

" hearty

" hearty friend to the diffenting intereft, I
" cannot, however, omit the prefent op-
" portunity of declaring, that I do by no
" means approve the conduct of thofe of
" *my own perfuafion*, who take a malicious
" pleafure in continually expofing the de-
" fects of the religion of their coun-
" try, and *in pouring out uncharitable cen-*
" *fures againft thofe* who fupport and de-
" fend it. Such a conduct as this, I am
" perfuaded, can anfwer no good purpofe.
" Whilft I enjoy the advantages of a tole-
" ration; whilft I am permitted without
" moleftation to worfhip God in the man-
" ner I moft approve; I fhall think my-
" felf bound by the laws of candour, of
" moderation, and even of gratitude, to
" refrain from faying, or doing any thing
" which may give *unneceffary* offence to the
" profeffors of that fyftem of religion,
" which the laws of this kingdom have
" countenanced and eftablifhed."

ANOTHER refpondent on a like occafion *, to his fentiments concerning the
proteftant diffenters, delivered with equal
freedom, adds—" Neverthelefs, I am fen-
" fible that thefe matters may appear in a

---

* Mr. *Gore.*

different

" different light to others of my fellow-
" chriftians. To them I willingly allow
" that liberty, which I take myfelf. Nor
" am I afraid or afhamed to profefs, that I
" highly difapprove of the conduct of
" *thofe*, who are continually inveighing
" againft eftablifhments in general, and
" *drawing odious comparifons between the*
" *members of the church of England*
" *and the Diffenters.* I am well perfuad-
" ed, that they *greatly injure* the caufe
" they mean to ferve; and that their con-
" duct in thefe refpects will anfwer no
" better end, than laying a foundation for
" enmity and uncharitablenefs amongft
" different parties of Chriftians. Whilft
" I am permitted to worfhip God accord-
" ing to the dictates of my own confci-
" ence, and publicly to avow my religious
" fentiments, I fhall account myfelf hap-
" py; nor fhall I ever think *meanly*, or *un-*
" *charitably*, of thofe, who can confcien-
" tioufly fubfcribe to articles of faith. I
" *entertain not the leaft doubt, that there*
" *are* MANY *fuch.*"

REMARKS

REMARKS

On Nº III.

" *So far only as she determines agreeable to the word of God.*] What doth such a determination as this amount to ?—Or, how can the church determine on any point for her members, under such a restriction ?—Is *she* the only proper judge of what is agreeable to the word of God ?—Or, hath not her members a right to judge, each for himself ?—If she may determine for her members, what is agreeable to the word of God, there is an end to the right of private judgement. On the other hand ; if every one of her members may judge for himself, what is agreeable to the word of God, then he may judge for himself, whether the church hath determined *so far only as is agreeable to the word of God.* And if he has a right to do this—to *judge* of the determinations of the church respecting religion,—he has a right to *act* agreeably to his own judgement; without which a right to private judgement can have no meaning, nor be properly reckoned any privilege to him. It follows, that he has a right to acquiesce in, or to deviate from the determinations of the church,

just

juſt ſo far as *he* may judge them to be agreeable or diſagreeable to the word of God.
In other words, the church hath not a
right of determining *at all* for her members, in the matter of religion. Her determinations may be *agreeable to the word
of God*; but, though they ſhould be ſo,
the requiring ſubmiſſion to them is never-
theleſs unwarranted by the ſame word of
God.

¹³ *The judgement of ſociety.*] I differ much
from our author in regard to the *propriety*
with which the writer here quoted has expreſſed himſelf. The judgement of *the
church* (for *her* right to determine for her
members is the point in queſtion) is chang-
ed for, the judgement *of ſociety.* Such
inaccuracies (I am willing to conſider this
as a mere inaccuracy) ſometimes entirely
ſhift the queſtion, and are always apt to
miſlead or confuſe the leſs cautious and
diſcerning reader.

¹⁴ *A judgement of diſcretion, or opinion.*]
If we admit this difference between theſe
rights, their coincidence in any other reſpect is not worth the mentioning. The
judgement of ſociety [the church] being a
judgement of *authority*, let the determinations thereof be ever ſo abſurd or iniquitous,
they

they muſt be obeyed. For " OBEDIENCE " and AUTHORITY are reciprocal terms. A " right in another to rule over us, and a duty " in us to ſubmit ourſelves, are but one and " the ſame thing differently expreſſed." ＊ It is true, " our thoughts are free, and our private judgement cannot be excluded by the deciſions of any authority upon earth." But, private judgement being no more than a judgement of diſcretion or opinion, we cannot avail ourſelves of it to any good purpoſe, nor exert it in action; and our thoughts being free can ſerve us but to brood over our religious thraldom. Our author had certainly loſt ſight of his own principles, when he exhibited the obſervations contained in this citation, as ſolid and juſt, or favourable to the rights of private judgement. To preſerve a conſiſtency in abetting the cauſe of religious liberty, it is neceſſary, that we avoid viewing the ſentiments of an author by the light in which he is held up to the public by perſons in authority. It ſeems to have been thought a recommendation of the paſſage we are conſidering, that the writer of it was *well eſteemed by a late* METROPOLITAN for his abilities in controverſial divinity.

＊ Dr. BALGUY's ſermon preached at *Lambeth-Chapel*, &c. publiſhed by order of the Archbiſhop, p. 1. *Davis* and *Reymers*, 1769.

Only

"*Only to forms and circumstantials, and matters of discipline.*] It is observed above by this same writer, that " the church hath a right of determining, *so far only* as she determines *agreeably to the word of God.*" And may not her determinations *in matters of discipline* be contrary to the word of God ?—They may. The determinations of the church of *Rome* on that head are many of them grossly so. It is not, therefore, a just distinction which is here made between *matters of doctrine, and matters of discipline,* by way of fixing the proper object of church-authority; and the truth is, the church hath not a right to determine for members *at all* what is, or is not agreeable to the word of God. That must ever be left to a man's own judgement and conscience. What the author of the *confessional* has remarked on this subject deserves great attention.— " There is not," he observes, " a word in the whole controversy concerning *church-authority* of a loofer and more equivocal signification than the word *discipline*. *Rites* and *ceremonies* are reckoned by some writers among the articles of *discipline*. And yet *rites* and *ceremonies* may be *idolatrous. Tests* and *subscriptions* are considered by others, under the notion of *discipline*; and thus the magistrate, upon the principles of the alliance,

alliance, [the church, upon the principles of the Rev. *W. Jones*] may have the power of *altering* doctrines. Bp. *Hoadley*'s state of the cafe prevents confusion. Wherever confcience is concerned, whether in matters of doctrine or difcipline, there all lawgivers or judges, Chrift alone excepted, are excluded." See *Conf. 3d edit. page* 61 of *Preface* to the *firft edition.*

REMARKS

On N° IV.

¹⁶ *I command thee, unclean fpirit,* &c.] This form of exorcifm *now* fhocks us. But is there not, in the office of ordination, a certain form retained at this day, which (in regard of the *power* affumed by the perfon who ufeth it) would appear equally fhocking, were it contemplated without any bias upon the judgement from the fanction of human authority ?—

¹⁷ *As if Chrift fhould fpeak the words out of heaven.*] His grace the late archbifhop of *Canterbury,* in his INSTRUCTIONS *to candidates for orders,* obferves, that, in uttering thefe words,—*Whofe fins* THOU *doft forgive they are forgiven: And whofe,* &c.—

· the

the bifhop doth not " pretend to grant *all*
" the powers, which the Apoftles had in
" this refpeçt." Is *any* power then, I would
afk, pretended to be granted to the candidate in this refpeçt, *viz.* of retaining and
forgiving fins ?—His grace mentions two
inftances of the efficacy of thefe words,
when pronounced by the bifhop. " When
" we ufe them, they give you, firft, an
" *affurance* that, according to the terms of
" that gofpel, which you are to preach,
" men fhall be pardoned, or condemned."
But do not thofe words give *equal* affurance,
whether they be pronounced by a *bifhop*, a
deacon, or even a *layman ?*—This is no
proof of *any* power being given to the
prieft of *retaining* or *forgiving fins*. " Se-
" condly," fays his grace, " they give you
" a right of inflicting ecclefiaftical cenfures
" for a fhorter or longer time, and of tak-
" ing them off; which in regard to exter-
" nal communion, is *retaining* or *forgiving*
" *offences*." But is it *retaining* or *forgiving*
SINS ?—Is the taking off an ecclefiaftical
cenfure, which had been inflicted, for inftance, upon an adulterer, to forgive the
man his SIN ?—Surely not !—God *alone*
forgiveth SIN, and he forgiveth it through
the man Chrift Jefus *alone*, and of the fame
affurance is given, and that, to *all* Chriftians, by the gofpel alone.—See *An* ANSWER

4   to

to *Letters concerning Confeſſions of Faith,*
&c. *Part* III. page 82, 83.——1769.

¹⁸ *Nor their act ſhould be of any force.*]
If this be ſo, what benefit doth a perſon ſo
abſolved receive?——He cannot receive any
comfort from the act of the miniſter, unleſs he himſelf be ſincerely repentant ; the
act being, in that caſe, confeſſedly of no
force. On the other hand, if he be repentant, and truſt in the mercy of God, he is
abſolved already *without* the miniſter's act,
who, in that caſe, hath no power to retain
the man's ſins by forbearing to pronounce
the ſentence of abſolution. Hence it appears, that the form of abſolution which is in
our office for the *viſitation of the ſick,* is not
calculated for adminiſtering any *true Chriſtian* comfort to the ſick perſon, while it may
lead him to depend, for the forgiveneſs of
his ſins, upon ſomething *beſide* the mercy of
God in *Chriſt Jeſus.*

¹⁹ *To every thing there is a ſeaſon,* &c.]
Yes ; and to ſome things there is *always* a
ſeaſon. And can our author ſpeak in ſuch
high terms of the preſent age, as being ſo
enlightened in compariſon of the times of
Cranmer, and yet doubt of the fitneſs of
the ſeaſon for the purpoſe of reformation ?——
Why talk of *ſubmitting to the wiſdom of our*
                                        gover-

governors, as to the PROPER TIME *for dismissing these encroachments upon Christian liberty ?*—If the requiring subscription to human articles of faith be really an *encroachment* upon Christian liberty, it will be an act of *justice* in our governors (what is here meekly stiled an act of *honourable indulgence)* to their subjects, to dismiss it; and for acts of this kind the *present* is surely the *proper* time. However, be this the *due* of their subjects, or only an *indulgence* to them, it is the part and duty of those who think it either, to *apply* for it, and a great impeachment of their *sense,* as well as of their *zeal* for the cause of reformation, to wait, without suit, the *offer* of it from government.

REMARKS

On Nº V.

²º *It is allowed on all hands,* &c.] But, " all the world knows," says a most ingenious writer, " the creed which goes " under the name of the Apostles, was " never penned by any of the Apostles. " The learned Dr. *Sykes* has proved that " one of its articles was not inserted till " the fourth century."—And he adds," For " my own part I shall make no scruple to " assert,

" affert, that it contains feveral grofs in-
" accuracies." *

" *And fo carefully tranfmitted*, &c.] But,
" it was rather too *hafty* a ftep taken by
" them, to draw up a fyftem of doctrines
" which fhould tie down the belief of
" their fellow-proteftants to the precife
" meafure and dimenfion of their own ;
" and efpecially fo as to *include pofterity* alfo
" in the ftrait inclofure." Vid. fupra,
N° IV. p. 93.

" *Subfcribe in any other fenfe whatever.*]
But if a fubfcriber to the articles is to interpret the articles *by fcripture*, how are they
explanatory of fcripture ?—And what fatisfaction do our governors receive from us,
when we fubfcribe, that we hold the true
doctrine of fcripture, if fubfcription be not
the teft of our interpreting fcripture, by
the fenfe given of it in the articles fubfcribed ?—" Whatever," fays our author,
" is the *true original* fenfe of fcripture
" herein" [the doctrine of *predeftination*,
for inftance] " THAT muft in courfe, and

---

* *Remarks upon the fecond and third of three Letters againft the* CONFESSIONAL, page 37.—*London :* Printed for *E.* and *C. Dilly,* in the *Poultry,* 1768.

M   " in

" in all reason and equity, be the sense in
" which I am to subscribe the article pro-
" posed."—If this be the true light in which
we are to view the *nature* and *obligation* of
subscription, what objection could be made
to subscribing any *popish* article of faith,
Transubstantiation, Purgatory, &c. ?—I am
not to subscribe these articles in *any other
sense whatever*, than the true original sense
of *scripture* herein. The sense of the *articles* may be quite *contrary* to the true original sense of *scripture*. With the true
sense of the *articles*, however, I have no
concern, but with the sense of *scripture*
therein. And if this be all the obligation
which subscribers to human articles of faith
come under, with what propriety and consistency doth our author call subscription to
them an *encroachment on Christian liberty*,
and plead so earnestly for *dismissing* it, as
such ?—(Nº IV. p. 102.)

" *What will be the consequences?*] The
conversion of the Christian ministry into a
political priesthood.

REMARKS

R E M A R K S

On N° VI.

²⁴ *A proper note*] Well worthy the particular attention of Dr. *Balguy*, and his an-
tagonist, Dr. *Priestly*, and by which both
of them may greatly profit. And I cannot
but wonder, that our author, in remarking
upon Dr. *Balguy*, should not have availed
himself more than he has done, of the
judgement and *caution*, as well as candour
and moderation, with which this note is
penned. " An attempt after all," speaking
of a reform of our ecclesiastical establishment, " it must be confessed, it is of no
" very flattering aspect with regard to the
" secular views of a member of the church.
" This is indeed so evident, that it might
" be expected that every candid judge would
" naturally ascribe it to a just emulation to
" discharge one's duty, with a conscience
" void of offence towards God and men, and
" a calm contempt for every other ambiti-
" on. A concurrence, it seems, of certain
" circumstances may disqualify a man from
" seeing it in so favourable a light. Should
" a person," continues this polite remarker,
" so

" fo fituated affect to queftion the con-
" fiftency of fuch an attempt with *the*
" *principles of juftice and honour* ;—he may
" be queftioned in his turn, whether it
" would be more *juft and honourable* for a
" fincere, though perhaps over-fcrupulous
" conformift, *to renounce all communion at*
" *once, and declare open war, as an alien,*
" with that church, which upon the whole
" he infinitely prefers to all others, which
" he means to ferve with his beft abilities,
" tho' *without any pretence to infpiration,*
" or infallibility, and of whofe wifdom he
" thinks too reverently, to fuppofe it un-
" willing to accept the moft effential fer-
" vice of any hand, but that of a profeffed
" adverfary. V. Sermon preached at the
" confecration of the Bifhop of *Landaff,*
" by Dr. *Balguy,* archdeacon of *Winchefter,*
" p. 20.

" How far the cenfure, in the paffage
" here alluded to, was meant to be extended
" by the refpectable writer, it is not eafy to
" guefs. An intrepid but too precipitate
" champion for the diffenters, (Dr. *Prieftly)*
" inveighs *outrageoufly* againft it, as expreffive
" of the genuine fenfe and fpirit of our
" church-eftablifhment in particular, and in-
" deed of all eftablifhments in general. If
" after

" after all we may be permitted to underſtand
" this paſſage, (as perhaps the worthy wri-
" ter himſelf intended it,) as directing its
" whole force againſt thoſe only, whoſe
" capricious and diſorderly conduct really
" defeats every good purpoſe of uniting in
" a religious community; its conſiſtency
" with the amiable principles of modera-
" tion, which he has publicly profeſſed
" upon other occaſions, will be the more
" indiſputable. Unluckily it is ſuppoſed
" equally to ſtrike at thoſe, who with all
" due humility claim a right of examining
" into the merit and propriety of thoſe
" eſtabliſhed regulations, to which they
" in the mean time punctually, though
" not implicitly ſubmit.—So at leaſt his
" expert antagoniſt is pleaſed to underſtand
" it, without which it might well defy the
" keeneſt edge of his argument or. in-
" vective."

** *Concerning the dropping of ſubſcriptions,*
&c.] A writer of *Three Letters to the Author
of the Confeſſional* makes the hackneyed objection againſt dropping ſubſcription to *human* articles of faith, and ſubſcribing to the
ſcriptures as the only rule of faith, (the
propoſal made in the confeſſional) *viz.* that
popiſh teachers and *fanatics* would in that
caſe find an opportunity of getting into

the

the church and venting their wild notions.
In anfwer to this it is judiciously obferved
by the *remarker*, "that no popifh prieft can
" fubmit to the propofal made in the *con-*
" *feffional*, of fubfcribing to the fcriptures
" as a full, perfect, abfolute, and compleat
" rule of faith, without making at the
" fame time a folemn renunciation of po-
" pery. As to *fanatical* preachers," continues he, " I beg leave to afk, whether fub-
" fcribing to the 39 articles has ever, or
" doth at prefent exclude any of them from
" our pulpits?—I would alfo afk him,
" whether there are no *cther* wild notions
" befides fuch as are condemned by the ar-
" ticles of the church of *England*?—But
" to be a little more particular, there are
" two kinds of enthufiafts : The one is to
" be met with in every age, and feems to
" be compofed of men of a warm imagi-
" nation, ftrong paffions, and little or no
" judgement. Whatever fuch men take
" in hand they always confider it as a mat-
" ter of the greateft importance. When
" religion is the object of their attention,
" we generally find them laying hold of
" fome tenet that will afford them an op-
" portunity of exercifing the powers of
" the imagination. Men of this ftamp
" are to be found in every denomination :
" And the fources of fuch an enthufiafm
" are

" are so numerous, that the proposing of
" confeffions of faith as an expedient to
" get rid of them, shews about as much
" wisdom as if a man were to make a pro-
" posal for containing the *Thames* in a blad-
" der. Had *Molinos* been a member of
" the church of *England*, in all probability
" he would have written the *Serious Call*.
" But there is another species of enthu-
" siasts, that rarely make their appearance
" in civilized countries; but are the off-
" spring of ignorance and barbarism.
" Active, and intrepid, they dream dreams,
" and see visions. Favoured with imme-
" diate illuminations from heaven, they
" soar above the vulgar rules of morality,
" and sanctifying the means by the end,
" omit nothing to compleat their defigns.
" Against such kind of men what would
" subfcriptions avail?—The eternal salva-
" tion of mankind is concerned—He is
" the anointed prophet of the almighty—
" His commiffion is supernatural—To him
" subfcriptions to articles eftablifhed by
" human authority, are like chaff before
" the wind. From hence we may difcern
" the inutility of them in both cafes. In
" the former cafe we have an evil, againft
" which we muft feek for relief in the
" principles of legiflation. If a man be
" infpired to commit murder, raife a rebel-

" lion,

" lion, or violate any of the fundamental
" laws of fociety, I know of no other, nor
" better remedy, than for the civil magif-
" trate, infpired by the *providence of go-*
" *vernment*, to punifh him according to the
" *tenor and purport* of fuch laws.

" BUT this inquiry into the confequence
" of abolifhing fubfcription is not altogether
" a matter of fpeculation, but depends, in
" fome meafure, upon experience. In-
" ftead then of giving way to the fug-
" geftions of fancy, let us follow this flow,
" but certain guide, and fee how the affair
" ftands in thofe churches where fubfcrip-
" tions are never mentioned but with the
" utmoft contempt.

" I AM informed, that in the County Pa-
" latine of *Lancafter* there are no lefs than
" forty congregations of proteftant diffen-
" ters. In *Yorkfhire* their number may be
" double. In all thefe focieties, and many
" others in different parts of the kingdom,
" their minifters are chofen without any
" fubfcription whatever. And I have not
" been able to learn, that one popifh prieft
" is to be found among them. And as to
" fanaticifm, perhaps no fet of men in the
" world was ever more free from it. It
" were to be wifhed that the letter-writer
" would

" would condefcend to examine things with
" a little more accuracy, and argue from
" faets; and not place fuch an implicit de-
" pendance upon the chimeras of his own
" brain."

²⁶ *In the power of the former,* &c.] Our
author plainly refers to our *ecclefiaftical* governors, in whofe power, however, it certainly is *not* to afford us relief in the matter
of fubfcription. It is folely in the power
of the *Britifh Parliament* to do this, and it
is not improbable, that the farther reformation of our ecclefiaftical eftablifhment
would have taken place before this time, if
the idea of the power of the bifhops in
this refpect had not been induftrioufly mag-
nified, and the abfolute neceffity of their
concurrence at leaft, in the enterprize, been
artfully fuggefted by thofe, who are inte-
refted to defeat every attempt in favour of
religious liberty. "Let the leading men,"
fays the very fenfible and fpirited author of
*Remarks upon the Firft of Three Letters to
the Author of the Confeffional,* " begin with
" making a *modeft,* but *earneft* application
" to *Parliament,* fetting forth the difficul-
" ties under which they labour, and the
" injury the proteftant religion daily re-
" ceives from confeffions of faith impofed
" by human authority, and let them petition
" to

" to be relieved from them. And should
" their requeſt be refuſed (which is not
" very probable) let them unite in openly
" proteſting againſt extending the ſubſcrip-
" tion to any articles, but thoſe that con-
" cern the true confeſſion of the Chriſtian
" faith, and the due adminiſtration of the
" Sacraments.

" WHEN they have ſo done, the world
" will be inclined to believe that they are
" in earneſt in their endeavours to promote
" religion. But if we take an attentive
" view of the ſtate of the times, we ſhall
" find no reaſon to ſuppoſe, that the great
" council of the nation would reject any
" attempts to reform the church, eſpeci-
" ally if ſuch propoſals were ſeconded by
" any number of the clergy."

²² *Than by dropping ſubſcriptions altoge-
ther, &c.*] PROPOSALS for an application
to *Parliament* for relief in the matter of
ſubſcription have been lately ſubmitted to
the conſideration of the *Engliſh* clergy *. In
conſequence of thoſe propoſals a meeting of
the clergy was requeſted, and held on the

---

* Sold by *B. White, Fleet-ſtreet*; *E.* and *C. Dilly*, in the
Poultry, &c. See ADDENDA.

17th

17th of *July* in the present year 1771 *,
when, as hath been mentioned in the public prints, they were unanimous in their refolutions, and appointed a Committee to
draw up a Petition previous to the next general meeting, which is fixed for *Wednefday*
the 25th of *September* next enfuing. In a
moft fpirited LETTER † to the Reverend
Dr. *James Ibbetfon*, from a *Clergyman of
the Church of England*, I am particularly
pleafed to find the *object* of this affociation
publicly avowed, and reprefented in fuch a
light, as feems fufficient to obviate every
cavil and infinuation againft the plan, and
the projectors and favourers of it: " I will
" tell you and all the world", fays this ani-
mated advocate for the caufe of religious
freedom, " that the prefent union againft
" *fubfcription* is directed to that *one point*
" *only*—that the rational fpirits now ce-
" mented for that purpofe throughout the
" nation, mean not to object to the Li-
" turgy, or any part of it—they will ap-
" ply for relief to that authority which
" alone can give it, to that authority, which
" impofed fubfcription—and they will ap-
" ply in the moft dutiful manner.—They
" wifh to be freed from the *unneceffary* bur-

* At the *Feathers* Tavern, in the *Strand*.
† *London*: Printed for S. *Bladon*, in *Pater-nofter-Row*,
1771.

" then

" then upon the conscience, of *subscribing*
", to the truth of all those human proposi-
" tions which the law obliges them to use ;
" and the man, who understands what *pro-*
" *testantism* is, will see, that a petition of
" such a sort will come with as much pro-
" priety from one who believes all that he
" subscribes, as from one who has his
" doubts."

Our request being so reasonable in itself
— the mode of preferring it being unex-
ceptionably proper and perfectly legal —
and determined as we are to shew ourselves
dutiful and respectful in our address to the
SUPREME power, what have we to do but
to wait the issue with a becoming confidence
in the wisdom and justice of a *British* and
protestant Legislature; making our suit in
the mean time to *Him*, in whose rule and
governance are the hearts of all men, that he
would so dispose and govern the hearts of
our rulers, that they may consult *the ad-*
vancement of his glory, the good of his church,
the safety, honour, and welfare of our So-.
vereign and his kingdoms; that all things
may be so ordered and settled by their endea-
vours, upon the best and surest foundations ;
that peace and happiness, truth and justice,
religion and piety may be established among us
for all generations.

T H E   E N D.

ADDENDA.

ADDENDA.

PROPOSALS

FOR AN

Application to PARLIAMENT for Relief in the matter of Subfcription to the Liturgy and Thirty-nine Articles of the eftablifhed Church of *England*.

Humbly fubmitted to the confideration of the learned and confcientious Clergy of the faid Church.

GENTLEMEN,

THE cafe of Subfcription to doctrines and forms of worfhip, compofed by fallible divines, and enjoined by human authority for public ufe, has been fo often and fo particularly examined and debated, that there feems to be very little room for new information on the fubject.

THE

THE principle upon which the Proteftant reformation from Popery was undertaken, conducted, and juftified, is, that " Holy " fcripture contains all things neceffary to " falvation, fo that whatfoever is not read " therein, nor may be proved thereby, is " not to be required of any man, that it " fhould be believed as an article of the " faith, or be thought requifite or neceffa-" ry to falvation *."

CONCERNING what is or is not *read* in the Scriptures, there can be no great diffi-culty. The point chiefly to be confidered by the fincere Proteftant, is, what may or

---

* In the Statutes given by Queen Elizabeth to Trinity College, in the Univerfity of Cambridge, the following Oath is appointed to be taken by every Fellow in the Cha-pel before his admiffion : " I, N. N. do fwear and pro-" mife in the prefence of God, that I will heartily and " ftedfaftly adhere to the true Religion of Chrift, and " prefer the Authority of Holy Scripture before the opi-" nions of men, that I will make the word of God the " Rule of my Faith and Practice—and look upon other " things which are not proved out of the word of God " as Human only. That I will readily with all my power " oppofe doctrines contrary to the word of God—That " in matters of Religion I will prefer Truth before " Cuftom—what is written before what is not writ-" ten."

See Introduction to CLARKE's *Scripture Doctrine of the Trinity.*

may

may not be *proved* thereby. Concerning which, amidst the great variety of doc- trines which occur in the course of every Clergyman's studies, difference of judge- ment is natural and unavoidable.

On these disputable points, the original Protestant principle reserves to every man his right of private judgement. In form- ing this judgement rightly, every man's con- science must be concerned; and if he meets with a doctrine which, after diligent and impartial examination, he believes *may not be proved* by Scripture, his conscience will require him not to subscribe or assent to that doctrine, *as such.*

Had this been duly considered by our first Protestant reformers (who strenuously and uniformly asserted the right of private judgement, in opposing their Popish adver- saries) they would more readily have per- ceived that the establishment of the doc- trines they agreed upon in the year 1552, might, in its consequences, infringe upon that valuable Protestant privilege on which they founded the propriety of their dissent- ing from the Church of *Rome,* and in the event, derive upon them, and their suc- cessors, the reproach of overturning their own principles, and requiring of *their* dis- ciples,

ciples, what they would not fuffer him, whom, with refpect to a *Primacy of order*, they allowed to be the firft Bifhop of *Chriftendom*, to require of *themfelves*.

ARCHBISHOP *Cranmer* was no more infallible than Pope *Leo* X. He could not be certain that every man equally learned, and equally honeft with himfelf, would fee the fcriptural proofs of *his* articles as clearly as he fuppofed he himfelf faw them. *Parker*, his Proteftant fucceffor, made confiderable alterations in *Cranmer*'s fyftem. And *Laud*, as every one knows, had his objections to *Parker*'s. And through all fucceeding times, from the firft uniformity-act under Queen *Elizabeth*, to the prefent hour, there have been leading divines, and among them not a few Bifhops, who in their refpective works have *occafionally* proved points by Holy Scripture with a mafterly precifion, which all the wit and learning in the world can never make to agree with fome of *Parker*'s articles.

THE authority of Synods, Convocations, or other humanly authorifed Affemblies of divines, is of no more validity againft the Proteftant principle (the right of private judgement) than the authority of a *Cranmer*, or a *Parker*. We have the united teftimony,

teſtimony of both theſe Reformers, that
" General Councils, even when gathered
" together by the commandment and will
" of Princes, (foraſmuch as they be Aſſem-
" blies of men, whereof all be not govern-
" ed with the Spirit and Word of GOD)
" may err, and ſometimes have erred, even
" in things pertaining unto GOD." [The
Latin hath it, *etiam in his quæ ad normam
pietatis attinent.*] " Wherefore things or-
" dained by them, as neceſſary to ſalva-
" tion, have neither ſtrength nor authori-
" ty, unleſs it may be declared that they
" are taken out of the Holy Scripture."
[The Latin ſays, *niſi oſtendi poſſint e ſacris
literis eſſe deſumpta.*] The premiſes being
equally true of national or provincial Synods, the concluſion is equally ſtrong
againſt them, as againſt General Councils.
And the queſtion once more recurs, *Who
ſhall be the judge?* The anſwer of the Proteſtant is, *Every man for himſelf.* My vote
for a Convocation-man cannot transfer to
him the right of judging for me. In matters of faith and ſalvation, no man can have
a Subſtitute or a Repreſentative.

WE have indeed been told, that the
Church of England does not propoſe all
her articles to be ſubſcribed as points neceſſary to ſalvation. But one would be
glad

glad to know where She draws the line, or
makes any diftinction to this effect. In her
XXXVIth Canon she enjoins *all and every
of thefe articles* to be acknowledged *ex animo* and fubfcribed, as *agreeable to the word
of God.* In her Vth Canon she enacts that,
" If any man shall affirm that thefe arti-
" cles are, in *any part*, erroneous, he shall
" be excommunicated *ipfo facto*." That is
to fay, (as we are informed by her own
Canonifts) " accurfed, devoted to the De-
" vil, and feparated from Chrift, and his
" Church's communion." See *Godolphin*
Repert. Canon. p. 625, 626. Is this an
adequate punifhment for thofe who diffent
from her in points *not neceffary to falvation?*

It is natural, Gentlemen, to fuppofe,
that you, to whom this paper is addreffed,
not only fee, but inwardly feel the incongruity of requiring of you this implicit
fubfcription, when compared with the liberty wherewith Chrift hath made us free,
and the general principles of the Proteftant
reformation. It is highly probable, that
you do not find *all* the eftablifhed doctrines
and forms of worfhip, to which you are
obliged by law to fubfcribe, in perfect
agreement with your private fentiments.
And where you find they are not, the integrity of your own hearts, and your defire
to

to edify the people committed to you, as
public teachers, in truth and fincerity, muft
difpofe you to wifh to be delivered from
this yoke of bondage, which every honeft
man, who after an impartial and diligent
ftudy of the Scriptures, differs from the
public Syftem, muft bear with reluctance
and regret.

In our prefent circumftances, the only
attempt we can make to be relieved from
this real grievance, is to apply by a decent
and dutiful Petition to the Legiflature, to
have it removed.

Our Ecclefiaftical Governors having de-
clined * to lend their hand towards our obtaining any relief (even the leaft relaxation

---

* See, Free and Candid Difquifitions prefented and de-
dicated to our Governors in Church and State; a Letter
to Abp. Herring, in the Year 1754, now made public;
&c.—The open and hearty Concurrence, however, of our
prefent worthy Church-Governors, would doubtlefs give
fingular Pleafure to every Friend of religious Liberty, and
(it is humbly prefumed) be no difcredit to themfelves.
A Remarker upon the Proposals hath taunted the
worthy Perfons who were prefent at the firft Meeting with
the *fmallnefs* of their Numbers and their *inconfiderablenefs*
in Station. This is the more to be lamented. Where the
reflection lies, muft be fubmitted to a more fair and impartial Public.

of

of this hard and illiberal condition of our being admitted Minifters in a Chriftian and Proteftant church) on the plea, that the matter is intirely in the hands of the Civil powers, have left us only to hope, that they will not oppofe our reafonable and righteous endeavours to help ourfelves.

THE only objeftion that has been made on the part of our Church.Governors (at leaft the only one worth notice) is, that if the Clergy fhould be releafed from their obligation to fubfcribe to the XXXIX articles, the Church would want fufficient fecurity of the *Orthodoxy* of her Minifters. But *Orthodoxy*, we apprehend, is a term which, in the mouth of a Proteftant, fhould only mean, an agreement in opinion with the Scriptures. And for the proof of fuch Orthodoxy, fufficient provifion feems to be made, in the fecond queftion put by the Bifhop to every Candidate for Prieft's or-ders, at the time of his ordination *.

THE.

---

* Queftion. Are you perfuaded that the Holy Scriptures contain fufficiently all doctrine required of neceffity for eternal Salvation through faith in Jefus Chrift ? And are you determined, out of the fame Scriptures, to inftruct the people committed to your charge, and to teach nothing as required of neceffity to eternal Salvation, but that which you fhall be perfuaded may be concluded and proved by the Scripture ?

Anfwer.

THE great difficulty in framing and forwarding a Petition to Parliament for the relief in queſtion, will ariſe from the diſperſion of the Clergy who wiſh for it, in different and diſtant parts of the kingdom, who are thereby diſabled (at leaſt the major part of them) by low circumſtances and other impediments, from meeting together and concerting meaſures for effecting ſo deſirable a deliverance.

To obviate this, and other inconveniences, which may ſeem, on a ſuperficial view, to attend an application of this nature, it is humbly propoſed,

1. THAT a few worthy and reſpectable Clergymen, reſiding in, or within miles of the Metropolis, who are diſpoſed

Anſwer. I am ſo perſuaded, and have ſo determined by God's Grace.

We have been lately informed that in ſome manuſcript notes on the Liturgy, &c. intituled, — "Amendments humbly propoſed" [by the late Dr. *Clarke*] "to the conſi-" "deration of thoſe in authority," a Copy of which is preſented to the Britiſh Muſeum, the following Query is put at the Head of the 39 articles. "Would it not be of" "ſervice to religion, if all Clergymen, inſtead of ſub-" "ſcribing to the 39 articles, were required to ſubſcribe" "only to the matters contained in the queſtions put by the" "Biſhop (in the Office for Ordaining Prieſts) to every" "perſon to be ordained Prieſt?"

N 3 to

to forward a Petition to Parliament for the purpofe abovementioned, fhall meet together, and confider of a proper time and place for a General meeting of their like-minded brethren, within the faid Metropolis *.

2. THAT previous to the public notice for fuch General meeting, fome eminent counfellor fhall be confulted, and requefted to give his advice in what manner fuch General meeting may be procured and conducted without offence, or without infringing the Laws of this country; and particularly, to give his opinion whether the Eftablifhed clergy (under the degree of Bifhops) are folely and fingly, of all his Majefty's Subjects, precluded from the right of petitioning Parliament with refpect to hardfhips and grievances attending their particular calling.

3. THAT the plan of a General meeting being thus fettled, public notice fhall be given of the time and place of affembling.

---

* Since the firft printing of thefe propofals, a meeting of the Clergy, &c. refiding in or near the metropolis, has been advertifed for the feventeenth of July.

4. THAT

4. THAT at the firſt General meeting, ſuch Clergymen being preſent, as are willing and deſirous to forward a petition to Parliament for relief in the matter of Subſcription, ſhall ſubſcribe their names to a paper purporting to be [Qu. aſſociation] a liſt of ſuch Clergymen as are diſpoſed to apply to Parliament for ſuch relief; which paper ſhall be kept by a proper perſon for the purpoſe of being ſubſcribed by any Clergymen who chuſe it at any ſubſequent General meeting, or during the intervals of the General meetings hereafter mentioned : and all perſons ſubſcribing their names to the ſaid paper, *and no others*, ſhall be conſidered as aſſociated members of, and admitted to conſult, ſpeak and vote in the ſaid General meetings.

5. THAT at the firſt General meeting a Committee ſhall be choſen out of the aſſociated members by ballot, not exceeding the number of which Committee ſo choſen, ſhall chuſe a Chairman to preſide at their reſpective meetings, and likewiſe at each General meeting, and alſo ſhall appoint from among themſelves ſuch perſon or perſons as may be able and proper to execute the office of Secretary, &c. to the ſaid Committee, and the ſaid General meet-

ings.

ings. This is neverthelefs propofed with all deference and fubmiffion to the fenfe of the firft General meeting, concerning the manner of electing their Chairman and other perfons qualified and proper to act in any capacity for the purpofes of continuing, adjourning, and otherwife regulating, fuch General meetings, and tranfacting the bufinefs thereof, fo long as may be necef-fary.

6. THAT a Petition to Parliament fhall be prepared by the faid Committee againft the fecond General meeting, fetting forth in the moft refpectful and dutiful terms the hardfhip, incongruity, and inconvenience of requiring Subfcriptions to the prefent eftablifhed forms, of the Proteftant clergy of this realm, and praying fuch relief herein. as to the wifdom of the Legiflature fhall feem meet.

7. THAT the draught of this Petition fhall be laid before the fecond General meeting, and fubmitted to the infpection and judgment of the affociated members then prefent, and fuch alterations made therein as the major part thereof fhall approve.

8. THAT the draught of the Petition being

being thus approved, shall be fairly en-grossed for Subscription, and shall be forth-with printed, and copies thereof sent by the associated members to the Clergy of their acquaintance in the Country respectively, requesting that the said Petition may be communicated to their Neighbours of the Clergy, and the sentiments of as many of their Brethren thereupon as can be had, sent up to their respective correspondents of the association, to be communicated to the General meeting, with power to such cor-respondents respectively to subscribe the names of so many of the country Clergy, as approve of the proceeding, to the said Petition.

9. THAT to give time for the several answers to be received from the country, the General meetings shall be adjourned from time to time, (the intervals not to exceed fourteen Days) during the space of six [eight or ten] months, after which it may be supposed the sense of so many of the Clergy in different parts of the king-dom as are disposed to join in or forward such Petition, may in a great measure be known.

10. THAT a Book or Books be provided to enter and record the whole proceedings,
as

as well of the General meetings, as of the
feveral Committees, to be depofited hereafter in fome public Library or Mufeum,
to perpetuate the memory of fo important
a tranfaction, that whatever may be the
event, our fucceffors may fee, there have
not been wanting, among their brethren,
men who employed their beft endeavours
to obtain relief from a grievance by which,
it may well be fuppofed, many more have
been diftreffed for two centuries paft, than
have been willing to complain.

11. THAT before the expiration of the
faid fix [eight or ten] months, (fome worthy member or members of the Honourable
Houfe of Commons being prevailed with to
prefent the faid Petition) fix of the affociated
members and no more, fhall be chofen by
ballot at a General meeting to attend the
Honourable Houfe with the faid Petition,
and then the Event fubmitted to the providence of a good and merciful GOD, and
the wifdom and piety of a Chriftian and Proteftant Legiflature, to whom may GOD in
all things give the fpirit of underftanding
and the fear of the LORD through JESUS
CHRIST. Amen.

A SUM-

A
SUMMARY VIEW
OF THE
LAWS relating to SUBSCRIPTIONS, &c.
WITH REMARKS,
Humbly offered to the Confideration of the
BRITISH PARLIAMENT.

[A] IN the Year 1553, were publifhed by the
King's Majefty's authority, "Articles
" agreed upon by the Bifhops and other learn-
" ed and godly men in the laft Convocation
" at *London*, in the year of our Lord 1552,
" to root out difcord of opinions, and efta-
" blifh the agreement of true religion."
Bifhop *Sparrow's* Collection of Articles, &c.

Remark.—It is however certain, that thefe
Articles were not agreed upon *in Convocation.*
Archbifhop *Cranmer's* account of the matter
was this. " I was ignorant of the fetting to of
" that title, and as foon as I had knowledge
" thereof, I did not like it; and when I com-
" plained thereof to the Council, it was an-
" fwered by them, That the Book was fo en-
" titled, becaufe it was fet forth in the time of
" the Convocation." *Burnet's* Hift. Reform.
Vol. III. p. 210, 211. And *Fox's* Martyrolo-
gy.——Bifhop *Burnet* fays, " It feemed to be a
" great want, that this".[the publication of thefe
Articles]

Articles] " had been fo long delayed, as the
" old Doctrine had ftill the *legal* authority of
" its fide." What *legal* authority the old Doctrine had, except in the decifions of foreign
Canons which were received in this Kingdom
with great refervation of municipal Rights, &c.
is not clear. The danger of dogmatizing was
not unknown in thofe days, and it would have
anfwered the end of the new Eftablifhment juft
as well to have enjoined Subfcription to the
Article cited below in the Remark upon D
only.

[B] A Mandate bearing date *June* 19, in
the feventh year of the King's reign [1553]
was iffued, addreffed to the Officers of the
Archbifhop of *Canterbury* [*Cranmer*] (refer-
ring to a previous Mandate addreffed to the
Archbifhop himfelf, and giving him authority to expound, publifh, denounce, and
fignify the faid Articles to the King's clergy
and people within his jurifdiction) to fum-
mon or peremptorily admonifh all and fingular Rectors, Vicars, Prefbyters, Stipendia-
ries, Curates, Rural Deans, Minifters, Mafters of Grammar Schools, public and private Preachers of the Word of God, Lecturers and all who exercifed any Ecclefiaftical
function of whatever denomination, includ-
ing even Churchwardens, to appear at *Lambeth*, on *Friday* the 23d day of *June*, between the hours of feven and nine, to do
and

and receive what may be farther agreeable to reason, and becometh their duty to the royal dignity. *Burnet's* Hist. Reform. vol. III. Collection p. 202.

Rem. This Mandate was issued pursuant to a Letter of the Archbishop's to the King and Council, " defiring that all Bishops might have authority from the King to cause all Preachers, Archdeacons, Deans, Prebendaries, Parsons, Vicars, Curates, with all their Clergy, to subscribe the said Articles."—The reason given by the Archbishop for such his defire was, " that " he trufted such a concorde and quietnefs in " Religion should shortly follow thereof, as elfe " was not to be looked for of many Years." Probably the good man found this expedient did not answer his expectation. For tho' his Powers by this Mandate were very full, we find him declaring at his Examination before *Weston*, that *he compelled no man to subscribe*. A Declaration that sufficiently shews, he had met with opposition to this measure of *Peace* and *Quietness*. And most probably it was not only the gentlenefs of his own difposition, but the consciousnefs of the incongruity of such compulsion, with the original principles of the Protestant Reformation, which occasioned his Forbearance. This is one instance of those difficulties the first Reformers found in accommodating the new Establishment to the temper of the times consistently with their own Professions of being determined in matters of Faith and Doctrine, by the Scriptures only. It is hardly necessary to observe,

obferve, that fuch Expedients are not only ufelefs now, but highly difparaging to the improvements we pretend to in the prefent times.

[C] A particular Mandate to the Bifhop
of *Norwich*, bearing date *June* 9, directing
him to caufe the faid Articles to be fubfcribed by every manner of perfon prefented unto him to be admitted to any Ecclefiaftical Order, Miniftry, Office, or Cure
within his Diocefe, and if any man in that
cafe fhall refufe to confent to any of the
faid Articles, and to fubfcribe the fame,
then his Majefty willeth and commandeth
him the faid Bifhop, that neither he, nor
any for him, or by his procurement in any
wife, fhall admit fuch recufant or allow him
as fufficient or meet to take any Order, Miniftry, or Ecclefiaftical Cure. For which
his fo doing, his Majefty promifes to *dif-
charge* the Bifhop from all manner of pe-
nalties or dangers of actions, fuits, or pleas
of *Premunire, Quare impedit,* or fuch like.
Burnet, Ibid. p. 203.

Rem.—Here was a ftretch of the Royal Prerogative which the end propofed would hardly
juftify. It was depriving the fubject of the benefit of the Law by an arbitrary *Non obftante.*
A writ of *Quare impedit* is a writ of *Right,*
and, without the Royal interpofition, would
have compelled the Bifhop to give the Clerk
inftitution,

inftitution, without fome better Reafon for denying it, than that the Clerk refufed to fubfcribe thefe Articles.

[D] A Mandatorial letter from the Bifhop
of *Ely* (Goodricke) Chancellor, and three
more appointed vifitors of the Univerfity of
Cambridge, dated *June* 1, 1553, addreffed
to Dr. *Sands* (probably Vicechancellor) and
to the Regents and Non-Regents of the faid
Univerfity, enjoining an oath to be taken
and fubfcribed by every Candidate for a degree in Divinity, or in Arts, containing,
among others, the following engagement,
Deinde me Articulos de quibus in Sinodo Lon-
dinenfi Anno Domini 1553. *ad tollendam opini-*
onum diffenfionem, et confenfum veræ Religionis
firmandum inter Epifcopos et alios eruditos vi-
ros convenerat et Regia Authoritate in lucem
editos, pro veris et certis habiturum, et omni
in loco tanquam confentientes cum verbo Dei
defenfurum, et contrarios Articulos in Scholis,
et Pulpitis vel refpondendo vel concionando op-
pugnaturum. Burnet, ubi fupra, p. 205.

Rem.—In the former part of this oath the
Candidate fwore, *fe veram Chrifti religionem om-*
ni animo complexurum, Scripturæ authoritatem
Hominum judicio præpofiturum, regulam vitæ et
fummam fidei ex verbo Dei petiturum. Cætera
quæ ex verbo Dei non probantur, pro humanis et
non neceffariis habiturum. It was utterly inconfiftent

fiftent with the man's profeffing thefe things, to
affert, that he would efteem thefe Articles for
true and certain, and to defend them as fuch
againft all mankind, upon the mere prefump-
tion that they were agreeable to the word of
God.

[E] Upon Queen Elizabeth's acceffion,
an Act of Uniformity paffed, wherein is no
mention made of Subfcription either to the
Liturgy eftablifhed by that Act or to any
Articles of Religion, nor in the vifitatorial
Articles of Inquiry of the fame year, is
there any one intimating that fuch Subfcription was required. See *Sparrow*'s Collection.

Rem.—It is remarkable that by this Statute,
the Clergyman offending againft it, is to be
lawfully convicted according to the Laws of
this Realm, by verdict of twelve men, or by
his own confeffion, or by the notorious evidence
of the fact; and was not left folely to the
Bifhop or Ordinary either for his trial or his punifhment; and as the words " and be thereof
" in form aforefaid lawfully convict," or words
equivalent, run through the whole Act, it was
manifeftly the intention of the Parliament to
put the inferior Clergy on the footing of the
reft of the free Subjects of the Realm, and not
leave them to the arbitrary cenfures of their refpective Ordinaries, as thefe were too apt to en-
croach upon the civil powers, by exercifing
their

their jurifdiction, where the laws of the Realm
fhould have reftrained them, complaints of
which were frequently made in Parliament, during this reign, and particularly with refpect
to Subfcription, as will be feen by and by.
N. B. There is one inflance of a trial by Jury
upon this Statute, before Lord Chief Juftice
Catlin, Bifhop *Sandys*, &c. preferved in a Book,
called *Part of a Regifter*, &c. p. 105. The Cul-
prit was one *Robert Johnfon*, Preacher at *Nor-
thampton*. He was indicted for adminiftering
the wine at the Communion without the words
of Confecration, for marrying without the Ring,
and baptizing without making the Sign of the
Crofs. He was convicted of the firft offence,
fentenced to fuffer a year's imprifonment, and
died in the Gate-houfe before the end of the
year, *viz.* 1573. In the courfe of the Trial,
and from the circumftances of *Johnfon*'s Defence, fome points of Doctrine were difcuffed,
and *Johnfon* was faid to defend a horrible Herefy, which was probably the chief inducement
with the Jury to find him Guilty. For the
Fact, as *Johnfon* fhewed, was not againft the
Order of the Book. Subfcription was hotly
urged this year. But *Johnfon*'s notion of the
words of Inftitution, was not provided againft
in the Articles.

[F] In the year 1562. King Edward's
Articles were revifed, and altered, fome
things added, others taken away, and the
number reduced to thirty-nine. At the
end of which, is the following Ratifica-

O   tion.

tion. " This Book of Articles before rehearfed, is again approved, and allowed to
be holden and executed within the realm,
by the affent and confent of our Sovereign Lady *Elizabeth,* by the Grace of God
of *England, France* and *Ireland* Queen, De-
fender of the Faith, *&c.* Which Articles
were deliberately read, and confirmed again
by the Subfcription of the hands of the
Archbifhop and Bifhops of the upper
Houfe, and by the Subfcription of the
whole Clergy of the nether Houfe in their
Convocation in the year of our Lord 1571."

Rem.—The Latin Articles of 1562, differ
very much from thofe [Latin] Articles publifhed by Convocation in 1571. It is probable
there was the like difference between the Englifh
copies, nor is it poffible now to know which of
them is authentic. The Bifhops and Clergy in
1562, fubfcribed Archbifhop *Parker's* Latin copy, and it is likely they fubfcribed a Latin copy revifed, in the Convocation of 1571. But the
Act of Parliament of that year refers to an Englifh book, and how that copy agreed with that
now in ufe, is totally unknown. It may be
faid however with great truth, that, on account
of the abovementioned differences, the articles
now fubfcribed, are not the Articles agreed
upon in the Convocation of 1562. There is
likewife a fallacy in the *Ratification* as it ftands
at prefent, with refpect to the Queen's confent,
as if both books of Articles were precifely the
fame,

fame, and equally *approved* by her Majefty; whereas the words fubjoined to the Latin Articles of 1562, fo far as the Queen's authority is concerned, are thefe, *Quibus omnibus Articulis fereniffima Princeps Elizabeth, Dei gratia Angliæ, Franciæ et Hiberniæ Regina, fidei Defenfor, &c. per feipfam diligenter prius lectis et examinatis, fuum affenfum præbuit*; which her Majefty might do without impofing Subfcription to them on her fubjects.

[G] In the year 1564 were publifhed, Advertifements partly for due order in the public adminiftration of the Sacraments, and partly for the Apparel of all perfons Ecclefiaftical. The Title of the laft fection is, " Proteftations to be made, pro-
" mifed and fubfcribed by them that fhall
" hereafter be admitted to any office, room
" or cure in any church, or other place
" Ecclefiaftical." Under this Title are the following Proteftations; " I fhall not preach or publicly interpret, but only read what is appointed by public authority, without fpecial licence of the Bifhop under his Seal. I do alfo faithfully promife in my perfon—to obferve, keep and maintain fuch order and uniformity in all external Policy, Rites and Ceremonies of the Church, as by the Laws, good Ufages and Orders, are already well provided and eftablifhed." *Sparrow's* Collection.

Rem.—

Rem.—What is here provided againſt, by this Proteſtation and Subſcription, was in a great meaſure ſecured by the Act of Uniformity, ſave in the Article of preaching and interpreting, concerning which there ſeems to have been no Law or Ordinance in being at that time, except the Queen's Injunctions of 1559; which were not underſtood then to have the force, or to make a part of the Laws of this Realm. Theſe advertiſements ſeem to have been calculated by Archbiſhop *Parker* to take the Clergy intirely into the hands of the Biſhops. What oppoſition theſe Advertiſements met with in the Queen's Council and elſewhere, and how diſtaſteful they were to many conſiderable men in different departments, may be ſeen in *Strype*'s Life of Archbiſhop *Parker*, Book 2. chap. xx.

[H] In the year 1571, An Act of Parliament paſſed injoyning Subſcription in theſe words; "Every perſon under the degree of a Biſhop which doth or ſhall pretend to be a Prieſt or Miniſter of God's Holy Word and Sacraments, by reaſon of any other form of inſtitution, confecration or ordering, than the form ſet forth by Parliament in the time of the late King of moſt worthy memory, King *Edward* the ſixth, or now uſed in the reign of our moſt gracious Sovereign Lady, before the feaſt of the Nativity of *Chriſt* next following, ſhall in the preſence of the Biſhop

or

or the Guardian of the Spiritualities of
some one Diocese, where he hath or shall
have Ecclesiastical living, declare his affent, and subscribe to all the Articles of
Religion, which only concern the Confession of the true Christian Faith, and the
Doctrine of the Sacraments, comprised in
a Book imprinted, intitled, *Articles whereupon it was agreed,* &c. and shall bring
from such Bishop or Guardian of Spiritualities in writing, under his Seal authentic, a Testimonial of such his Assent
and Subscription, and openly on some *Sun-
day* in the time of the public service afore-
noon in every Church, where, by reason
of any Ecclesiastical living he ought to
attend, read both the said Testimonial and
the said Articles, upon pain that every such
person, which shall not before the said
feast, do as is above appointed, shall be
ipso facto deprived, and all his Ecclesiastical promotions shall be void, as if he then
were naturally dead." *Statutes* 13 *Eliz.*
c. 12.

Rem.—The noble stand made by the House
of Commons in the reign of Queen *Elizabeth*
on divers occasions against Ecclesiastical encroachments, and in favour of Religious liberty, plainly shews, that the limiting the Subscription of the Clergy to such Articles " as
only concern the Confession of the true Christian

O 3   faith,

faith, and the doctrine of the Sacraments," in this Act, was no idle provision, or words without meaning. Much has been said concerning the uncertainty, what Articles were not to be subscribed under this restriction, and an argument has been drawn from thence for an unlimited Subscription. It appears however from the Conversation between Archbishop *Parker* and Mr. *Peter Wentworth* in 1571, that the Articles for the Homilies, Confecrating of Bishops and such like, were put out of the book, and were doubtless struck out in the copy annexed to the Bill. And as that copy is now irrecoverable, and as it hath been said, separated by some unfair practice from the Act which refers to it, the Clergy must be left to their own judgement, which of the Articles are or are not excepted in the Statute. Some learned and worthy persons have thought that Subscription to the 6th and 25th Articles is sufficient to satisfy the intention of the Legislature, the rather as the article which concerns the Homilies was certainly intended to be left out ; and therefore as most of the doctrinal articles are but abridgements of what the Homilies treat of at more length, the House of Commons had no more time to examine those Articles how they agreed with the word of God, than they had to examine the Homilies, as both must have been examined together. It is only necessary to observe farther, that whatever Articles were enjoined by this Act to be subscribed, the same and no other were to be read and assented to, as prescribed by the

subsequent

subsequent Sections of this Statute. See *D'ewes's* Journal, p. 239.

[I] In the same year (1571.) the Bi-shops put forth a Collection, intituled, *Liber quorundam Canonum Disciplinæ Ecclesiæ Anglicanæ, Anno* 1571. in which, under the Title *de Episcopis,* it is ordained, that persons approved for public preachers, should have their Licences renewed, *ita tamen ut prius subscribant articulis christianæ religionis publice in Synodo approbatis, fidemque dent se velle tueri et defendere doctrinam eam quæ in illis continetur ut consentientissimam veritati verbi divini.* And under the Title *Concionatores,* there is the following injunction. *Et quoniam articuli illi religionis christianæ in quos consensum est ab Episcopis in legitima et sancta synodo, jussu et authoritate serenissimæ principis Elizabethæ convocata et celebrata haud dubie collecti sunt ex sacris literis veteris et novi Testamenti, et cum cælesti doctrinâ quæ in illis continetur, per omnia congruunt; quoniam etiam liber publicarum precum, et liber de inauguratione archiepiscoporum, episcoporum, presbyterorum et diaconorum, nihil continent ab illa ipsa doctrina alienum, quicunque mittentur ad docendum populum, illorum articulorum, authoritatem et fidem, non tantum concionibus suis, sed etiam subscriptione confirmabunt. Qui*

O 4 *secus*

ſecus fecerit, et contrariâ doctrina populum turbaverit, excommunicabitur. Sparrow's Collection.

Rem.—The intention of theſe Injunctions for Subſcription to the Articles, was to ſupply, what the Biſhops thought the Parliament had left ſhort, namely, to require a Subſcription to *all* the Articles, as appears by their making the Subſcriber aſſert their agreement with the word of God, and particularly mentioning the Book of Conſecrating of Biſhops, &c. It is however certain, that the Queen never gave her Sanction to theſe Canons, and *Grindal* then Archbiſhop of *York* " doubted whether they had *vigorem legis*," [which out of all doubt they had not] " and " thought the Queen's *verbal* aſſent would not " ſerve them, if they ſhould be impleaded in " a Caſe of Premunire," in which he was very much in the right.

[K] In the year 1584. the Biſhops and Clergy of the Province of *Canterbury* aſſembled in Convocation, put forth a Collection intituled, *Articuli pro Clero*, in which it was injoyned, that no Biſhop ſhould thereafter admit any perſon to Holy Orders, except he was of his own Dioceſe, &c. *vel ſaltem, niſi rationem fidei ſuæ juxta articulos illos Religionis in Synodo Epiſcoporum et cleri approbatos latino ſermone reddere poſſit, adeo ut ſacrarum literarum teſtimonia quibus*
eorundem

eorundem Articulorum veritas innititur reci-
tare etiam valeat. Sparrow's Collection.

Rem.—Archbishop *Whitgift* was now promoted to *Canterbury.* His predecessor *Grindal*
had complained greatly of the ignorance of the
Clergy, and had used his utmost endeavours to
supply the Church with abler men; but generally without effect. By this time, it is likely,
the Bishops began to see the impropriety of requiring Subscription of poor Curates and Candidates for Orders to a set of Articles of which
they knew so little; and to obviate any reproach
that might arise from this practice, enjoined the
examination mentioned in these Canons. And
had they stuck to this expedient, it may easily
be imagined they must not have ordained a
Tithe of the Candidates who aspired to the
Priesthood. Perhaps very few at this day
would undertake to recite the testimonies of
Holy writ, on which the truth of these Articles depends. The Spirited Commons, however, became sensible of this arbitrary impositi-
on, and in the Parliament of 1585 petitioned
the House of Lords, among other matters relating to the Church, " That for the encourage-
" ment of many to enter into the Ministry
" which are kept back by some conditions of
" Oaths and Subscriptions whereof they make
" scruple, it may be considered, whether this
" favour may be shewed them, that hereafter
" no Oath or Subscription be tendered to any
" that is to enter into the Ministry, or to any
" Benefice with Cure, or to any place of preach-
" ing

" ing, but such only. as be expresly prescribed
" by the Statutes of this Realm; save only that
" it shall be lawful for every Ordinary to try
" any Ministers presented to any Benefice
" within his Diocese by his Oath, whether he
" is to enter corruptly or incorruptly into the
" same." *D'ewes's* Journal, p. 358. It is humbly presumed, that the Answer of the Archbishop of *York* to this reasonable Petition, is far
from being satisfactory upon Protestant principles.

[L] In the year 1597 were put forth,
Capitula sive Constitutiones Ecclesiasticæ, by
the Archbishop, Bishops, and Clergy of the
Province of *Canterbury* assembled in Con-
vocation, said in the Title-page to be con-
firmed under the Great Seal of *England*.
In this collection, the requisite qualifica-
tion of Ministers, so far as relates to the
Articles, is prescribed in the same words.
Sparrow's Collection.

Rem.—By this time Archbishop *Whitgift* had
so far established his power that all opposition
to his system of Discipline became fruitless even
in Parliament. *Strype* relates that, " a great
" heap of Grievances in the Church were thrown
" into the Parliament [of 1597] by Bills put in
" by divers persons; but were not read, by
" means, no doubt, of some higher influence."
Among others, " A grievance no way inferior
" to the former the ungodly use of the Statute
" of

" of 13 *Eliz.* concerning Faith and Sacraments,
" by which men are forced to Subfcription,
" and forced to accufe themfelves," i. e. by declaring their diffent from fuch Articles as did not
concern Faith and Sacraments. N. B. Thefe
Canons were confirmed under the Great Seal,
and they feem chiefly to aim at reforming fome
abufes in the Ecclefiaftical courts ; by way, one
may fuppofe, of precluding enquiries into fuch
matters, in Parliament. *Strype's* Life of *Whitgift*, p. 509.

[M] IN the year 1603, the Convocation
compofed the Book of Canons now in ufe,
the thirty-fixth of which injoyns Subfcription, 1. To the King's Supremacy. 2. To
the Book of Common Prayer, as containing
in it nothing contrary to the word of God.
3. To the thirty-nine Articles, acknowledging all and every the faid Articles to be
agreeable to the word of God. Which
Subfcription is to be made in this form of
words, " I *N. N.* do willingly and *ex
animo* fubfcribe to thefe three Articles abovementioned, and to all that are contained in
them." The Royal affent to thefe Canons
is attefted under the Great Seal of *England* *.

Rem.—It is queftionable how far thefe Canons
are binding. Some great authorities fay, they have
no force with refpect to the Laity, and that they
bind the Clergy only by virtue of their Oath of

* See the G R A C E annexed.

Canonical

Canonical obedience, which however is limited to *things lawful and honeſt*, and what is *lawful* and *honeſt* in Canonical commands or injunctions cannot *in equity* be determined before the Perſon againſt whom the crime of diſobedience is committed. It is againſt the principles of juſtice, and the genius of the Britiſh conſtitution, that the ſame man ſhould be both judge and party. Prohibitions from the temporal Courts lye againſt the Courts eccleſiaſtical, in caſes which concern the Clergy as well as the laity. Why ſhould not the caſe of this Canonical Subſcription (as the temporalities of beneficed Clerks are *now* made to depend upon a compliance with it) be ſubject to the verdict of twelve men, as other caſes of leſs importance are made to be, by the Act 1. *Eliz.* cap. 2 ? Very many of theſe Canons are totally fallen into diſuſe, on account of the impracticability of carrying them into execution. Others, which might be executed, are wholly neglected, poſſibly becauſe the execution of them might ſet the exerciſe of Canonical diſcipline in ſo many trifling matters, in too odious a light. But can any thing be more odious than to compel a learned and Proteſtant clergy to ſubſcribe implicitly to all theſe antiquated propoſitions, on the pain of being excluded from the benefit of any temporal emolument in the Church, where they might be of the greateſt uſe to the people ?

[N] In the year 1613. A Grace was paſſed by the Univerſity of *Cambridge*, in conſequence of Letters from King *James* I. pre-

prefcribing Subfcription to the three Articles in the 36th Canon to the Candidates for the Degree of Batchelor of Divinity, and of Doctor in each faculty *.

[O] In the year 1616, the King *(James I.)* fent directions to Dr. *John Hill*, then Vice Chancellor, and the Heads of Houfes in the Univerfity of *Cambridge*, fignifying his pleafure that he would have *all* who take any degree in the Schools, to fubfcribe to thefe Articles.

Rem.—Remarks on thefe Royal Directions, will be found under the Letter [S].

[P] In the year 1628 King *Charles* I. caufed the 39 Articles to be republifhed, prefixing thereto a *Declaration*, prohibiting the leaft difference from the faid Articles, and configning thofe who fhould affix any new fenfe to any Article to the Church's cenfure in his Majefty's Commiffion Ecclefiaftical, declaring that his Majefty would fee due execution done upon them.

Rem.—Nothing can be more inconfiftent than to continue this Declaration at the head of the 39 Articles, while every Subfcriber is, by Canon 36, confined . to a particular invariable form of words, in expreffing his affent and confent to

* See the G r a c e annexed.

them;

them, nor can any judgment be made, where an article is ambiguously expressed, which of the senses given to it by different interpreters, may be called *drawing it aside from the plain and full meaning thereof:* Nor is the punishment threatened, for offences against this declaration, now possible to be executed, as, thanks be to God and a virtuous Legislature, the Commission ecclesiastical, to which the Offender is consigned for his censure, is no longer in being.

[Q] In the year 1640 were framed by the Archbishops, Bishops, and Clergy in Convocation, Constitutions and Canons Ecclesiastical, in the sixth of which an Oath is injoyned to be taken by all Archbishops and Bishops and all other Priests and Deacons, all Masters of Arts (the Sons of Noblemen only excepted) all Batchelors and Doctors in Divinity, Law or Physic, all that are licensed to practise Physic, all Registers, Actuaries and Proctors, all Schoolmasters, all such as being Natives or naturalized, do come to be incorporated into the Universities here, having taken a degree in any foreign University, " that they approve the Doctrine and Discipline or Government established in the Church of *England,* as containing all things necessary to Salvation." *Sparrow's* Collection.

Rem.—For the objections made to this arbitrary

trary oath, See *Fuller*'s Church Hift. xi. Book, p.
170, 171. And *Heylin*'s Life of Archbp. *Laud*,
p. 443.

[R] December 16: 1640. Upon a debate in the Houfe of Commons concerning
thefe Canons, it was refolved, *nemine Con-
tradicente*, " that the Clergy of *England*
convened in a Convocation or Synod, or
otherwife, have no power to make any Con-
ftitutions, Canons. or Act whatfoever in
matter of Doctrine, Difcipline or otherwife, to bind the Clergy or Laity of the
land, without common confent of Parliament." And at the fame time it was un-
animoufly refolved " that thefe particular
Canons do contain in them matter contrary
to the King's Prerogative, the fundamental
Laws and Statutes of the Realm, to the
Rights of Parliament, to the property and
liberty of the Subjects, and matters tending to fedition, and of dangerous confequence." *Rufhworth*, Vol. IV. p. 112.

Rem.—This Refolution moft certainly repro-
bated the Canons of 1603, as well as thofe of
1640. The former, any more than the latter,
never had any common confent of Parliament.
It is in vain to pretend that this vote was paffed
in times of irregularity. The forms of Parliament
were never more folemnly or religioufly obferved: and, as it feems, this refolution is not at all
different

different from the language of the Statute 13
Car. 2. chap. xii. wherein it is said, that nothing
in that Statute shall be construed " to confirm
" the Canons made in the Year 1640, nor any
" of them, nor any other Ecclesiastical laws or'
" canons not formerly confirmed, allowed or
" enacted by Parliament, or by the established
" Laws of the Land, as they stood in the year
" of our Lord 1639." The Canons of 1603,
had no *establishment* but King *James's* License
and Ratification : and no less had the Canons
of 1640, the Licence and Ratification of King
Charles I.   And if ever the matter should come
to a fair Trial, King *James's* Canons could no
more stand before the established Law of the
Land, than those of King *Charles*.   And whatever authority one of these Princes derived from
the 25th of *Hen.* 8. the other had equally the
same.

[S] *January* 19 : 1640-41. " Upon Mr.
White's report from the Grand Committee
for Religion, it was resolved upon the question, that the Statute made about twenty-
seven years ago in the University of *Cambridge*, imposing upon young Students a
Subscription according to the 36th Article
of the Canons, made in the Year 1603, is
against the Law and Liberty of the Subject,
and ought not to be pressed upon any Student or Graduates whatsoever." *Ibid.* p. 149.

Rem:—From the manner in which this Reso-
lution

lution is expreſſed, it is probable the Caſe
ſtood thus. King *James's* Letters to the Univerſity required Subſcription of Batchelors in
Divinity and Doctors in each Faculty. This
became a *Statute*, but was probably extended to
other graduates *pro arbitrio*, and this being objected to, the Univerſity might apply in 1616
to the King for his *farther* pleaſure in this matter, and the affair coming before the Parliament
in 1640, they ſeem to have taken both orders together. Otherwiſe it is certain that the Statute
of 1613 extends to no *younger ſtudents* than
Batchelors in Divinity, and Doctors in each Faculty. But this is wholly conjectural. The material obſervation is, that the whole Practice is
juſtly and ſeverely condemned in a moſt wiſe and
righteous Parliament.

[T] In the year 1662. 13 & 14 *Car*. II.
was paſſed the laſt Act of Uniformity, by
which Subſcription to the Declaration of
Conformity to the Liturgy of the Church of
England, as by Law eſtabliſhed, is required
of every Dean, Canon, Prebendary of every
Cathedral or Collegiate Church, and of all
Maſters and other Heads, Fellows, Chap-
lains and Tutors, of or in any College, Hall,
Houſe of learning or Hoſpital, and of every
public Profeſſor and Reader in either of the
Univerſities, and in every College elſewhere,
and of every Parſon, Vicar, Curate, Lec-
turer, and of every other perſon in holy Orders, and every Schoolmaſter keeping any

public

public or private School, and of every perfon inftructing or teaching any Youth in
any houfe or private family as a Tutor or
Schoolmafter. And by the fame Statute
Subfcription unto the nine-and-thirty Articles mentioned in the Statute made in the
13th year of the reign of the late Queen
Elizabeth, is required of the Governor or
Head of every College or Hall in either of
the Univerfities, and of the Colleges of
Weflminfter, *Winchefter* and *Eaton*, and all
upon the pain of forfeiting their refpective
offices or preferments, from the Dean down
to the petty Schoolmafter.

Rem.—This vindictive Statute, having now
compleatly done its work, and occafioned fuch
a variety of diftrefs from the Reftoration to this
prefent hour, to fuch of the clergy as could not
affent to the principles of King *Charles* the fecond's Bifhops, may now, we hope, be foftened
and qualified, without any detriment to the
Church of *England*. Neither King, Lords nor
Commons have any thing to fear from the mu-
tinous fpirit of a peevifh, irritated and obftinate
generation of Nonconformifts. The Toleration
laws have rendered Proteftant Diffenters of all
Denominations, peaceable, rational and valuable
Subjects to the Civil Government; and the
Clergy of the eftablifhed Church, who folicit a
relaxation of their prefent bonds, derive their
pretenfions only from the original principles of
the Proteftant reformation, and thofe generous
maxims

maxims of Civil and Ecclefiaftical policy which give a fanction to the Revolution of 1688, and to the Settlement of the Crown in the lineage of our moft gracious Sovereign, to whom and his Royal Houfe they profefs the moft fincere and cordial attachment. They fly for affiftance on the prefent occafion to that auguft Body, who have ever been the Protectors of the Rights and Privileges of the *Britifh* Subject, and who have in many periods of our Hiftory, from the firft dawn of Reformation, fhewn their care and con-cern to deliver the pious and confcientious Clergy, not only from the oppreffions of the Ro-man Pontiff, but from the attempts and en-croachments of many in high places, whofe am-bition difpofed them to eftablifh the like ufur-pations, under a more plaufible pretext. The time is now come, they hope, when a candid hearing will be given to their reafonable and modeft Remonftrances, and all obftructions to their relief removed, which are founded in no-thing, but a defire of exercifing a defpotic Rule over the Confciences, or in pretended fears and apprehenfions of Confequences, which can have no place, where the freedom folicited has no other object than the promotion of peace and unity, virtue and true piety among Clergy and People in the prefent ftate of things, and the everlafting Salvation of all in the world to come.

THE

THE
ARTICLES

To be fubfcribed unto by all perfons, before they are admitted to any Degree;
with the G R A C E paffed in the year
1613, and King *James's* D I R E C-
T I O N to the V. Chancellor and
Heads of Houfes, enjoining Subfcription
to thofe Articles :

To which is added,

The R E S O L U T I O N of the Houfe of
Commons concerning the faid GRACE.

I. *Articles to be fubfcribed unto, &c.*

1. THAT the King's Majefty, under
God, is the only fupreme Gover-
nor of this Realm, and all other his Highnefs's Dominions and Countries, as well in
fpiritual or ecclefiaftical things or caufes, as
temporal ; and that no foreign Prince, Perfon, Prelate, State or Potentate, hath, or
ought

ought to have, any jurifdiction, power, fuperiority, pre-eminence or authority, ecclefiaftical or fpiritual, within his Majefty's
faid realms, dominions, and countries.

2. THAT the book of Common Prayer,
and of ordering of Bifhops, Priefts, and
Deacons, *containeth in it nothing contrary to
the word of God*, and that it may lawfully
be ufed, and that he himfelf will ufe the
form in the faid book prefcribed, in public
prayer and adminiftration of the Sacraments,
and no other.

3. THAT He alloweth the book of Articles agreed on by the Archbifhops and
Bifhops of both Provinces, and the whole
Clergy, in the Convocation holden at *London* in the year 1562. and that *He acknow-
ledgeth all and every the Articles therein contained* (being in number 39. befides the ratification) *to be agreeable to the Word of God.*

WE whofe names are underwritten do
willingly and *ex animo* fubfcribe to the *three
Articles* before mentioned and to *all things*
in them contained.

Excerpta è Stat. Acad. Cantab. p. 25.

P 3　　　　II. *The*

II. *The Grace by which Subscription to these
Articles is required of Candidates for the
Degree of Bachelor in Divinity, and of
Doctor in each Faculty.*

Jun. 2do, 1613. Placeat Vobis, ut juxtà
tenorem Literarum a Sereniſſimo Rege *Ja-
cobo* miſſarum, hoc in Senatu decernatur;
ut nullus in poſterum ſibi conceſſam hábeat
Gratiam pro Gradu Baccalaureatus in Theo-
logia, vel Doctoratus in aliqua Facultate
adipiſcendo, qui non priùs coram Domino
Procancellario, aut ejus deputato, tribus
Articulis, ſc. regii Primatus, Liturgiæ *Anglicanæ*, et Articulorum Religionis de quibus convenerunt Archiepiſcopi et Epiſcopi
A. D. 1572, propria manu ſua ſubſcrip-
ſerit. Et ut hæc conceſſio veſtra loco ſta-
tuti habeatur, et in libris Procuratorum in-
fra decem dies inſcribatur.

III. *King* James's *Direction to the* V. Chancellor and Heads of Houſes *in the Univerſity of* Cambridge, *given by himſelf to*
Dr. Hills, *Vice Chancellor*, &c. *on* Dec.
3. 1616, *at* Newmarket.

" His Majeſty ſignified his pleaſure that
" he would have all that take *any* degree
" in

" in Schools to fubfcribe to the three
" *Artitles*."

. AFTER fome other directions, the King
ordered " that Mr. V. Chancellor and the
two Profeffors of Divinity, or two of the
Heads of Houfes, do every *Michaelmas*,
when His Majefty reforts unto thefe parts,
wait upon His Majefty, and give Him a
juft account how thefe His Majefty's inftructions are obferved."

A COPY of thefe Directions written or
at leaft figned by the King himfelf, was
foon afterwards fent by the Bifhop of *Winchefter* to the V. Chancellor, with the following letter.

To the Right Worfhipful Dr. *Hills*,
Mafter of *Catherine Hall*, and V. Chancellor of *Cambridge*,

Good Mr. V. Chancellor,

I have fent you his Majefty's hand to his
own Directions. I think you have no pre-
cedent, that ever a King, firft with his own
mouth, then with his own hand, gave fuch
directions; and therefore you fhall do very
well to keep that writing curioufly, and the
directions religioufly, and to give his Majefty

4

jefty a good account of them carefully;
which I pray God you may; and fo with
my Love to yourfelf, and the reft of the
Heads, I commit you to God. From Court
this 12th day of *Dec.* 1616.

Your very loving Friend,

James Winton.

IV. *The Refolution of the Houfe of Commons
concerning the Grace paffed by the Univerfity of* Cambridge *in the year* 1613.

In the year 1640, upon the Report from
the Grand Committee of Religion, it was
refolved by the Houfe of Commons, " That
the Statute made about 27 years fince in the
Univerfity of *Cambridge,* impofing upon
young Scholars a Subfcription according to
the 36th Article of the Canons made in the
year 1603, is againft the Law and Liberty of
the Subject, and ought not to be preffed upon any Student or Graduates whatfoever."
Rufhworth's Hiftorical Collect. vol. 4. *p.* 149.

THE author of the Hiftory of the Puritans, after citing this Refolution of the
Houfe of Commons, takes notice, " that
about five months forwards they paffed the
fame refolution for *Oxford,* which was not
unreafonable, becaufe the *Univerfities* had
not

not an unlimited power by the 36th Canon
to call upon *all their Students* to subscribe,
but only upon such *Lecturers or Readers of
Divinity* whom they had a privilege of li-
cenfing ; and to this I conceive the laft words
of the Canon refer ; *if either of the Univerfities offend therein, we leave them to the danger of the law, and his Majefty's cenfure.*

" And it ought to be remembered, that
all the *proceedings* of the Houfe of Commons
this year in punifhing *delinquents*, and all
their *Votes* and *Refolutions* about the circumftances of public worfhip, had no other
view, than the cutting off thofe *illegal ad-
ditions* and *innovations* which the fuperftition of the late times had introduced, and
reducing the difcipline of the Church to
the ftandard of *Statute* law. No man was
punifhed for acting according to law ; but
the difpleafure of the houfe ran high againft
thofe, who in their public miniftrations, or
in their ecclefiaftical courts, had *bound thofe
things upon the Subject*, which were either
contrary to the laws of the land, or about
which the laws were altogether *filent*."
Neal's Hift. of the Puritans, vol. 1. 4to. *p.* 665.

The

*The Form of a Grace for the Removal of Sub-
scription to the three Articles contained in
the 36th Canon.*

PLACEAT vobis, ut illi, qui Munia Scho-
laftica in Regiis Statutis contenta expleve-
rint, in' pofterum fibi conceffam habeant
Gratiam pro Gradu in aliqua Facultate fuf-
cipiendo, etfi tribus Articulis in Canone tri-
cefimo fexto comprehenfis non fubfcrip-
ferint.

THIS GRACE was offered at *Cambridge*, on the 11th of *June* 1771.

www.ingramcontent.com/pod-product-compliance
Lightning Source LLC
Chambersburg PA
CBHW030107030726
47498CB00007B/2288